D1031813

THE BEATLES' SECOND ALBUM

Dave Marsh

Creem Editor and Best-Selling Author

RODALE

Rodale books may be purchased for business or promotional use or for special sales. For information, please write to:
Special Markets Department, Rodale Inc., 733 Third Avenue, New York, NY 10017

Printed in the United States of America
Rodale Inc. makes every effort to use acid-free ∞, recycled paper ♲.

Book design by Drew Frantzen

Library of Congress Cataloging-in-Publication Data

Marsh, Dave.
    The Beatles' second album / Dave Marsh.
        p.   cm.
    ISBN-13 978–1–59486–426–1 hardcover
    ISBN-10 1–59486–426–8 hardcover
    1. Beatles.   2. Rock musicians—England—Biography.
3. Popular music—1961–1970—History and criticism.   I. Title.
ML421.B4M186   2007
782.42166092—dc22   2007030598

Distributed to the trade by Holtzbrinck Publishers
2 4 6 8 10 9 7 5 3 1   hardcover

We inspire and enable people to improve their lives and the world around them

For more of our products visit **rodalestore.com** or call 800-848-4735

For Matt Orel . . . sparring partner

CONTENTS

1

GIVE THEM 22 MINUTES (THEY'LL GIVE YOU THE WORLD)

Yeah, yeah, yeah.

I can recite the case for the prosecution as well as anybody.

The Beatles' Second Album runs only 22 minutes. It contains just 11 songs. You might say the Beatles had nothing to do with it, since it folds into one disc tracks that have four or five discrete sources in the Beatles' "legitimate" UK catalog. Dave Dexter Jr., the Capitol Records executive who assembled the album, despised rock'n'roll as a whole, believing it inferior to what he called "legitimate" music. It's indisputable that the group came to hate the idea of Dexter's butchery.

Besides: It's full of songs the Beatles—who changed songwriting forever—didn't even write. The track selection relegates Paul to an incidental lead vocalist, as subordinate to John Lennon as George Harrison is. Ringo doesn't even have a featured spot. The mixing and mastering leave the soundscape as shoddy as if it had been filtered through damp cardboard; the stereo rendition is worse.

With the Beatles, the second album the Beatles made for Parlophone Records, released only in the United Kingdom, is well balanced artistically between original songs (eight) and cover versions (six) and between John's lead vocals and Paul's (with leavening from George and Ringo). Sonically, it was state of the art for 1964. Its 14 tracks run a combined 33 minutes.

On top of that, Capitol Records wrapped the *Second Album* in some of the cheesiest cover art of all time, worse than your average mid-sixties James Brown album. It's not even camp, it's just slapdash: A dozen photos of the Beatles on each side, cropped every which way (one consists in its entirety of Ringo's bangs, right eye, right ear, and nose), laid out in what seems to have been a single five-minute session. *With the Beatles* has a dignified, even intriguing light-and-shadow shot of the band. It is one of the defining images of their early career.

With the Beatles sports liner notes by Tony Barrow, the band's publicist; however callow, they are at least minimally informative. The back cover of *The Beatles' Second Album* displays the song titles in order; a plug for their first US album, *Meet the Beatles*; and liner notes that consist of five lines off a theater marquee, written in ascendingly greater size type from a tiny "Never before has show business seen or heard anything like them . . . " to a huge "The Beatles' Second Album." And in type about the same size as the copyright notice, "Produced in London by George Martin."

The Beatles' Second Album wasn't even the Beatles' second album—not in America or anywhere else. It came out in April 1964. In February, Vee-Jay Records had also produced an album of the group's early material, with a track listing that differed considerably from *Meet the Beatles* but also derived from the Parlophone masters. At about the same time, MGM Records issued *The Beatles with Tony Sheridan and Their Guests* using material the band recorded in Germany in 1961. On the five songs they play on (yes, the rest is material by some other band, not that MGM acknowledged it), the Beatles serve only as Sheridan's backing group on all but one track, "Cry for a Shadow."

So how can anybody love such an ungainly, fraudulent mess?

Because this brief album represents the Beatles of 1964, when they were unquestionably the greatest rock'n'roll band the world had ever seen. And it shows them, if not at their most shapely, at least with maximum brute force.

Because whatever Dave Dexter Jr.'s intent, those 11 songs told things about the band and its music, rock'n'roll, and the world in general that some of us desperately needed to hear. And this is the way it was presented to us, the material we were given to use in making sense of the new world the Beatles awoke.

Because no matter whether it "accurately" portrays its makers and their condition in April 1964, the *Second Album* creates an image of the Beatles that is, arguably, closer to who they were, underneath the collarless coats and the careful coifs, the well-scrubbed complexions and constant affections, than anything else that leaked out to America in those heady first months—even naked greed is allowed to raise its head.

Because some of what they didn't write had everything to do with what they did compose, then and in the future.

Because the ballad—"You Really Got a Hold on Me"—came from Smokey Robinson and the Miracles, not from a damnable Broadway show, like "Till There Was You," the ballad on *Meet the Beatles*.

Because if you let it, this music, arranged in this order, from the statement of purpose at the beginning to what may be the greatest rock'n'roll record they ever made at the end, will change your life.

It changed mine. Confessing this may rank with the goofier absurdities in the annals of rock criticism. Nevertheless, it's flat-out true.

For the past 43 years, *The Beatles' Second Album* has been, for me, a kind of lodestone. When it felt like the scent of freedom that leaped out at me from rock'n'roll and rhythm and blues had faded into the irrelevancies of the past, this record was one of the places where I could find refuge and reassurance. (Of course there are others. Anyone who tells you there is a single greatest rock'n'roll record either doesn't know enough to make the claim or doesn't love rock'n'roll enough to be worth listening to.)

Always, every single time I hear it, *The Beatles' Second Album* makes the case—and not in a nostalgic sense. It feels fresh and alive. When it plays, the atmosphere it creates reminds me not only that the past isn't even past, as William Faulkner said, but also that the past is more than a hint of the future, it is the passkey to reaching it.

———

There's a canyon of time to bridge here. To risk the ridiculous, the task I'm taking on is akin to what Thomas Mann faced in writing *The Magic Mountain*, where he tried to convey the consciousness of pre-1914 Europe to people who lived with the sensibility of post–World War I Europe. In an early passage in that book, Mann described the conditions under which he told his tale:

> The exaggerated pastness of our narrative is due to its taking place before the epoch when a certain crisis shattered its way through life and consciousness and left a deep chasm behind. It takes place— or, rather, deliberately to avoid the present tense, it took place, and had taken place—in the long ago, in

the old days . . . in the beginning of which so much began that has scarcely yet left off beginning. Yet it took place before that, yet not so long before. Is not the pastness of the past the profounder, the completer, the more legendary, the more immediately before the present it falls?

Yeah.

———

The conventional attitude toward *The Beatles' Second Album* is entirely an anachronism. Mostly, it presumes a degree of choice that nobody—not the Beatles, not the Beatles' audience, and not even Capitol Records—really had.

"Consumer advisory: *Seek out imports or reissues of albums with the original British track configuration*," wrote Robert Palmer in his 1995 *Rock & Roll: An Unruly History.* (His italics measure his intensity.) This advice and implicit criticism is aimed at just such albums as *The Beatles' Second Album*, though the examples he uses are the US editions of *Rubber Soul* and *Revolver*, whose bowdlerization was and is indefensible. In almost all cases, the process by which the 14 songs that were standard on UK albums were whittled down to the US standard of 12 (or fewer) was haphazardly done by people with no ear whatsoever for what might have been a group's musical breakthroughs or signature performances.

———

The Beatles' Second Album is truly a special case, for reasons that are complicated and trace back to this weird Dave Dexter Jr. character, whose influence on the band's career amounts to a kind of Forrest Gump effect. His genuine stupidity about musical quality and, for that matter, the future of Western civilization, time and again set up conditions under which the Beatles' American record catalog takes its odd shape, which leads to, among other things, one of the biggest breaches ever of the group's carefully manicured public image.

I couldn't really be bothered to defend the *Second Album* against the charge that it's a happy accident, though I might point out that so is *Casablanca*. Of course, the record does not at all reflect the Beatles' intention (though, as we shall see, I doubt that artistic intention drove the assemblage of *With the Beatles*, either).

I've written more than anyone about the struggle of rock musicians to acquire artistic freedom—to gain the right to have their output represent their own intentions—and what happens when they obtain it, fail to gain it, or squander it. This is a major theme in my books about Bruce Springsteen, Elvis Presley, the Who, and Michael Jackson.

But it's not the only theme, and it takes a backseat here to another story because in 1964, that kind of artistic freedom didn't exist yet because the Beatles hadn't created it. But even after it came into being, other things also mattered.

The value of *The Beatles' Second Album* is the value that album derives from the way that American listeners responded to it. In 1964, Robert Palmer's advice to seek out imports would have been gibberish. For me, and the great majority of Beatles fans, probably including Palmer, who at the time was a student at Little Rock University, there wasn't any way to get British albums, nor was there a pipeline to notify us of their existence. By the time *Rubber Soul* and *Revolver* were released a year or two later, that was no longer nearly so true. But it was true in 1964 and it was true for several years thereafter—perhaps until the late 1970s in many areas of the United States.

Many American editions of the Beatles' music aren't worth considering in building a chronology of how their music developed. But if all that mattered about the Beatles were the intentions and experiences of John, Paul, George, and Ringo, we would have a very different musical culture. It wouldn't necessarily be worse, but the discrepancy would be profound and those who lived in one world would have a good deal of trouble, all of it based on their own reliable preconceptions, communicating to those who lived in the other.

This book was written across just such a gap, a world in which reality did not encompass 21st-century commonplaces like ready access to recordings from every corner of the world. Rock criticism did not exist, nor did the idea that this kind of music even *might* be taken seriously as music, let alone as philosophy, passion, or signifier of adult identity. Nor did the idea that rock or any other music derived from African-American sources could become the dominant expression of Anglo-American— and even in some respects worldwide—musical commerce on a long-term basis. Nor did the idea that an album's worth of material, rather than a single song, was the proper way to evaluate recorded popular music. Enumerate those issues and you've begun to describe a situation very much like the one Mann was discussing.

I'm not arguing for the superiority of that older world, much less for its supposed "innocence." I'm pointing out that it existed and that to judge it by the conditions that obtain today is to guarantee false conclusions. In that world, not only could no teenager be expected to acquire a foreign recording, but, among many other incongruities, the performer had virtually no control over which of his recordings were issued; new styles of popular music and new stars were intended to be discarded within a few months at most; and an aesthetic rather than commercial rationale for popular vocal music existed entirely as rhetoric. No one who wanted to defend any part of that situation would write about the Beatles, who repudiated all of it and with glorious results, at least for Lennon, McCartney, Harrison, and Starr and their near-contemporaries.

So, by all means, buy and listen to the Beatles' albums in their native configurations, if you wish to hear them as the Beatles themselves expected they would be heard. But remember, if you take Robert Palmer's advice (and he was

9

as good at writing about American music as any writer, ever), you will not be buying a copy of "She Loves You," or most of the group's other singles. You won't get "I Want to Hold Your Hand," "Long Tall Sally," "I Call Your Name," "I Feel Fine," "Daytripper," "We Can Work It Out," "Paperback Writer," "From Me to You," or "This Boy."

You can get those on US CDs called *Past Masters Volumes 1* and *2*. In the British catalog, you can buy them on *Rarities*—a ludicrous title, because those songs are among the most popular and widely purchased in the history of recorded music, let alone the Beatles' catalog.

I'll tell you this: I would have been pissed off if I'd brought home *The Beatles' Second Album* and "She Loves You" wasn't there. And I have never believed for one millisecond that the discrepancy—theirs lacked it; ours had it—had at that time anything at all to do with what the Beatles intended. In Britain, it was considered poor value to ask fans to buy singles as LP tracks. It's a purely mercantile standard and can have very damaging artistic results.

———

The world moves on. But memory lingers and what it lingers upon is sometimes important to understanding where the world moved, and why, and how. It turned out, when I started talking to my contemporaries about what I was trying to do, that *The Beatles' Second Album* was important to a lot of people. Over dinner, I had to wrest the book back from my friend and colleague Greil Marcus before he could write it instead of me. John Sinclair, poet, rebel role model, and constant listener, said simply, "Oh, *yeah*!" Theirs weren't the only affirmations, but they provide the spectrum.

I can't promise you that what is important to me is what's important to Marcus, Sinclair, or other friends. CDs and LPs and 45s are solid objects but music is ethereal. But, while I take Palmer at his word, it seems likely to me that almost any American who lived with it in that curious year of 1964 and thereafter would have been overjoyed to hear the CD reissue of *The Beatles' Second Album* when it finally arrived in 2004 as part of the four-disc set, *The Capitol Albums Vol. 1.* Not because it gave the most accurate rendition of the Beatles making music in the studio, but because it gave such an accurate and impressive account of what the Beatles did to those of us who heard them and succumbed to their charm and power.

There's a story here. I mean to tell it. It has a beginning, a center, an aftermath. Much of the story concerns the Beatles; some of it concerns me; I hope that a lot of it applies to other people who lived through that merry cataclysm dubbed Beatlemania and came out of it transformed, however hard it may be to explain how.

When the cataclysm subsided, what we were left with pretty much traveled on a single track: the story of the

Beatles as a grand triumph of good cheer and fellowship, teen idols turned into heroic artists.

Because of all the contradictions of its creation, and because it unwittingly came closer to describing the shape of the Beatles' musical roots than anything else they did in the recording studio, *The Beatles' Second Album* tracks on several other levels. Also because of the response of fans now and the Beatles then to how it and its other bastard American brethren, spawned from greed and greatness in near-equal measure, because of what it says about who the Beatles could have been and what they were and who we could have been and what we were, too.

Maybe *With the Beatles* would have had the same effect. I can't figure it out and don't need to, because I know something more important: It wouldn't have made nearly so good a story. No writer needs to apologize for locating and treasuring one of those.

2

PLEDGE OF ALLEGIANCE

The Beatles' Second Album opens with "Roll Over Beethoven," an eight-year-old Chuck Berry song.

The Beatles' version is nothing much to brag about—this may be the weakest of the old rock'n'roll songs they ever recorded. The band gets the tempo about right, not careening out of control as most Berry acolytes do. The problems are all up top, and up top is pretty much all George Harrison.

Harrison's guitar playing is the main problem. He gets the opening Berry lick right; for the Beatles' shows in Liverpool and Hamburg, he had to play several of Chuck's songs on a nightly basis. But Harrison doesn't sound inspired, the way Keith Richards of the Rolling Stones sounded on such songs—Richards eventually evolved an entire style by elaborating on Berry's small set of riffs.

George sounds reserved singing the first two verses—like he's imitating John Lennon emulating Chuck Berry.

Like a lot of Berry songs, "Roll Over Beethoven" is relatively wordy—a lot of syllables are crammed into some of the measures—and the way George sings makes it feel like he's learned them by rote but doesn't have enough air left to supply much emotion.

Without a strong lead vocal, even Paul's lonely background "woo" sounds weak, especially compared to his perfect, exuberant "woo" in "I Saw Her Standing There." The one striking thing about the way George sings "Roll Over Beethoven" is that he sounds so English—but it's pretty obvious that wasn't the intent.

The track picks up some excitement during the bridge, when Ringo's drumming pushes the pace and John's rhythm guitar steps up the energy level. The solo that follows is competent though still without inspiration.

Harrison's singing on the final verse seems a little forlorn. He's basically hanging on for his life by the time he gets to the last "Dig to these rhythm and blues," which is supposed to provide the song's payoff, with the last guitar solo the cherry on top. The solo isn't bad, but it's patched on from another take, and obviously so—not even George Martin's usually meticulous editing is up to snuff on this track.

Stones bassist Bill Wyman once told me, "Keith had to teach George Harrison the guitar solo on 'Roll Over Beethoven' and then George still had to play it at half-speed." I doubt that (not the lesson, the half-speed business). But you wouldn't want to compare it with the

Beatles' version of Berry's "Rock and Roll Music," made at the end of '64 for *Beatles for Sale* (or in the US, *Beatles '65*). That one sports one John Lennon's scorched-earth vocals.

———

If "Roll Over Beethoven" is so weak, why does it lead off the *Second Album*? Here's where you can begin to see the way wires crossed between England and America, in this case with an assist from Canada.

In Canada, the Capitol Records affiliate, blessed with Paul White, an international A&R rep who loved the group, was quicker and more eager to release Beatles records than Capitol was in the United States. "Roll Over Beethoven" came out as a Canadian single in December 1963 and hit the charts in March 1964, just after the Beatles made their first trip to the States. The record was so popular there, it leaked over the border and placed at number 68 in *Billboard*'s Hot 100.

Capitol's Hollywood headquarters wanted to release the track as a single too, but George Martin persuaded them to substitute "Can't Buy Me Love," a new track and also the single at that time in the UK. Nevertheless, *Billboard* made a point of stating that "Roll Over Beethoven" would be on the Beatles' next album.

Whether or not the Beatles knew about the track's chart stature, "Roll Over Beethoven" is the song that opened their first US concert, in Washington, DC, just after their first American TV appearance on *The Ed Sullivan Show.*

Several performances of "Roll Over Beethoven" were taped or filmed, including one at the Star Club in Hamburg, just before the band cracked the British charts. The song appears in seven of the Beatles' many BBC broadcast performances, two of them from before the July 1963 studio session that produced the version on the *Second Album.* (The *Live at the BBC* CD has the version from late February 1964.) They played it at their Hollywood Bowl performance later that year, too.

Obviously, the song meant something to them, regardless of whether Canadians and Yanks cherished it. Then again, what those lyrics meant to the North American audience might have been pretty close to what they meant to the Beatles.

"Roll Over Beethoven" is a pledge of allegiance to rock'n'roll, one of the earliest and one of the best rock anthems ever. It's certainly the toughest such statement of faith. By declaring that his song is so good that it can make even the most revered of classical music's composers roll in the grave, Berry spits in the eye of the music's detractors.

He had every right to do so, since (as anyone who has ever essayed one of his songs knows) playing Chuck Berry songs is very easy and playing them correctly—with appropriate timing, intonation, and feeling—is extremely difficult. (Harrison actually came closer than most and, were he being compared as anybody but a Beatle, or on a song that was by someone else, his playing might deserve a good deal more sympathy.) But the haters of the Beatles and of rock'n'roll never recognized such qualities, trapped as they were in preconceptions about music itself.

———

In European classical music, harmonic development is pretty much the center of everything. Rhythmic elaboration is all but nonexistent and dissonance is more common and desirable than polyrhythm; even tempo exists in a pretty narrow range. This idea carries through the chamber music and symphonies of the ancien régime into the Tin Pan Alley, vaudeville, and Broadway songs of the early 20th century that are commonly revered as "standards"—the works of George Gershwin, Irving Berlin, Jerome Kern, Harold Arlen, and Richard Rodgers, among others.

African-American and Afro-Caribbean music, which are the source points for rock, place the focus on other elements, particularly rhythm and timbre. This is why rock'n'roll, even when played by whites, struck early listeners steeped in the other tradition as "Negro."

In the Northern Hemisphere, almost all musical education for decades, even centuries, assumed that the priorities of Europe were "correct." So the sneering began.

But if you fight your way through the preconceptions and begin to look through the other end of the telescope, an interesting thing happens. "My feeling is that if you want to listen to something primitive, you should listen to Mozart," said Robert Palmer in Ken Mandel's 1993 film, *Bluesland*. "Because if you hear Mozart, there's almost no rhythmic variation in it, it's 1-2-3-4 forever. No cross-rhythms or polyrhythms to speak of. The way that music's interpreted, all of the tonal qualities of the instruments tend to be very clean and pristine. There's no kind of textural variety like you would get in the blues, in terms of roughening the texture out on certain words, playing around with the pitch on certain words. Nothing like that in Mozart." Palmer, one of the great scholars of the musical interchange between Africa and the Western Hemisphere, says this deadpan, not to increase the irony but to emphasize that he's dead serious.

The great achievement of the Beatles was to balance those two perspectives, which is one reason you can argue that everything that the group took from black music—which was an enormous amount—they gave back in near-equal measure through their effect on black writers, performers, and producers such as Stevie Wonder, Sly Stone, Maurice White of Earth, Wind & Fire, and Philadelphia producers and songwriters Kenneth Gamble and Leon Huff.

But nobody commenting on the Beatles in 1964—or for about a decade beyond that—put together a case anything like Palmer's or, for that matter, mine. I'm not sure that even John Lennon, for whom songs like "Roll Over

Beethoven" represented a statement of both allegiance and identity, would have bought all of it.

Not that every "serious" music critic hated them. On December 29, 1963, Richard Buckles of London's *Sunday Times* even called them "the greatest composers since Beethoven."

When other classically oriented music critics tried to describe what the Beatles sounded like, they became lost in irrelevant detail. Most notoriously, critic William Mann in the *Times* of London on December 23, 1963, referred to their "natural use of the Aeolian cadence," which befuddled not only Beatles fans but Lennon, too. "To this day, I don't have any idea what [Aeolian cadences] are," John told David Sheff in one of his last interviews. "They sound like exotic birds."

Mann wrote a smart piece, praising the Beatles' acoustic guitar sound and vocal duets, and above all their composing, but cluttered his discussion with terms such as "flat submediant key switch" and "chains of pandiationic clusters," the purpose of which isn't really apparent. Well, yes, it might be: Its purpose is to exert control over musical discussion by using technical jargon that excludes those without a fairly high degree of musical education. There's always a simpler way to describe such things—by "Aeolian cadence" Mann seems to have meant a sustained C major chord—but if you talk like that, just about anybody can understand and challenge your ideas. Ultimately, if such a critic speaks of music in the vernacular, he's likely to wind up having to listen to Palmer's disquisition on the failings of Mozart. Or worse, having to respond to it.

Lennon told Sheff he traced the Beatles' acceptability to middle-class audiences to Mann's article but it not only wasn't that simple, it wasn't that easy. By the time Mann's review appeared, there had been no lack of comment upon the supposedly scurrilous nature of the Liverpudlians and all the things into which they breathed life: scads of rock bands, outlandish costume both on the stage and in the audience, and a weird "lack" of grooming. The Beatles fostered a culture where expertise was grounded not in studiousness but in activities—for example, not decorously listening to music, studying scores, and fastidiously picking over nuanced details, but making music by the sweat of one's brow, with an eye toward turning the audience into a frothing mass and lining one's pockets. In the Beatles' wake, bands sprouted by the hundreds, as if Johnny Lennon was an Appleseed who strewed guitar picks and drumsticks rather than seeds. All of them with an eye on the main chance, fame, fortune, and the hot little item in the front row.

Greil Marcus called it "a pop explosion. . . . Excitement wasn't in the air, it was the air." For their part, cultural guardians heard tom-toms from over the horizon, and they weren't wrong. Change was coming, faster than anyone expected.

The first thing that threw everyone off-kilter was that

the Beatles were not a fad. As Elvis's had, their popularity went on increasing month after month and, eventually, year after year. But there was no military conscription in England; the Beatles did not have a car wreck or an airplane crash; none of them married his teenage cousin, or got caught with an underage girl from over the border, or decided to become an evangelist. Whatever the opposite of a one-hit wonder was, they were that. Whatever the opposite of a short-lived teen idol was, they were that, too.

A good many were not pleased at this endurance, regardless of their overt politics. "The Mersey Sound is the voice of 80,000 crumbling houses and 30,000 people on the dole," wrote London's communist newspaper, *The Daily Worker*, in December 1963. The Beatles showing no particular allegiance to the working class (other than in their accent, demeanor, sense of humor, ambition, diet, greed, and choice of music), *The Daily Worker* had no particular use for them. Its article gave no sign that people from the Mersey working class finding a way to speak for themselves—about anything—might be an improvement over the class system that insisted there always was and always ought to be someone of superior mien, status, and wealth to speak for them.

But the reactions of British adults to the Beatles were fairly diverse. After the initial shock of the haircuts wore off, they didn't seem particularly exotic. Throughout the 20th century, many of the UK's best comedians had emerged from Liverpool. And coming up alongside the

Beatles were bands like the Rolling Stones, who managed to create from five relatively middle-class boys an image of truly determined delinquency (something like what John, Paul, George, and even Ringo were like before Brian Epstein dressed and groomed them). The mass appeal of the Beatles spread even to those of voting age.

In early 1963, Britain's ruling Conservative Party found itself in hot water over a sex-and-espionage scandal that resulted in the resignation of Secretary of State for War John Profumo over an affair he had with a call girl, Christine Keeler, who had connections to agents of the Russian government. It was also aboil because of a cooled-off economy. The Beatles initially provided a distraction from such woes, and by early 1964, the group had cracked the US market, with lovely implications for British foreign trade, especially since they recorded in America for a wholly owned subsidiary of a British company, EMI. Conservative Party members were given instructions to drop the group's name as often as possible in their speeches. The royal family got into the act, with the Queen Mother expressing amusement after seeing their set at the Royal Variety Performance, Princess Anne smiling her delight at the same show, and the Queen expressing interest in the frequency of Ringo's haircuts.

In February, William Deedes, the minister of government information services, who had been one of the Cabinet ministers who had been gulled by Profumo's assertion that he hadn't slept with Christine Keeler, made a speech pouring effulgent praise upon the Fab Four.

"They herald a cultural movement among the young which may become part of the history of our time," he said, adding, "For those with eyes to see it, something important and heartening is happening here. The young are rejecting some of the sloppy standards of their elders, by which far too much of our output has been governed in recent years. . . . They have discerned dimly that in a world of automation, declining craftsmanship and increased leisure, something of this kind is essential to restore the human instinct to excel at something and the human faculty of discrimination."

At this temporal distance, "discerned dimly" leaps out. Deedes wasn't about to state that the Beatles understood their own importance and power. That thought was unthinkable. They were not of a station to think such thoughts, and in any event, the comfort came from seeing them as a foreign-trade golden goose, not as leaders of a rejectionist insurrection. (Fortunately for his confidence, Deedes had not met John Lennon, for whom tweaking the noses of Tory cabinet ministers was a football match and mother's milk all in one. Fortunately for Lennon, or for his bank balance anyway, manager Brian Epstein kept such attitudes well in check, or at least cleverly disguised as mere cheek.)

Deedes, more than the Beatles or "Roll Over

Beethoven," incited arch-conservative pundit Paul Johnson to a tirade in the February 28 issue of the *New Statesman* entitled "The Menace of Beatlism." He delivered a fist to the jaw of Minister Deedes: "No doubt any public relations man, even a grand one who sits in the cabinet, can use a touch of credulity, but even so I remember thinking at the time: 'If Deedes can believe that, he'll believe anything.'" He made every effort to carve up the Beatles like the geese he presumed them to be, slashing about with phrases like "the monotonous braying of savage instruments," "the growing public approval of anti-culture," and "the indispensable teenager, who has, what is more, the additional merit of being a delinquent."

Johnson also claimed that "behind this image of 'youth,' there are, evidently, some shrewd older folk at work. . . . In any case, merit has nothing to do with it. The teenager comes not to hear but to participate in a ritual, a collective groveling to gods who are themselves blind and empty." Here, he sounds comically like latter-day rock and rap haters of the Wynton Marsalis and Joseph Lieberman ilk.

"If the Beatles and their like were in fact what the youth of Britain wanted, one might well despair," Johnson continued. "I refuse to believe it—and so I think will any other intelligent person who casts his or her mind back far enough. What were we doing at 16? I remember the drudgery of Greek prose and the calculus, but I can also remember reading the whole of Shakespeare and

Marlowe, writing poems and plays and stories. . . . At 16, I and my friends heard our first performance of Beethoven's Ninth Symphony; I can remember the excitement even today. We would not have wasted 30 seconds of our precious time on The Beatles and their ilk.

"Are teenagers different today? Of course not. . . . The dull, the idle, the failures: their existence, in such large numbers, far from being a cause for ministerial congratulation, is a fearful indictment of our education system. . . . The core of the teenage group—the boys and girls who will be the real leaders and creators of society tomorrow—never go near a pop concert. They are, to put it simply, too busy. . . . They are in the process of inheriting the culture which, despite Beatlism or any other mass-produced mental opiate, will continue to shape our civilization."

Ludicrous as such pronouncements now seem, they were stated in gentlemanly fashion. Johnson's almost visceral loathing for the working class and uneducated notwithstanding, he wasn't suggesting that the Beatles be run out of the country or that their records be burned or that their followers be punished for preferring that music. He assumed that the proper hierarchical natural order would restore itself soon enough and, in the meantime, it seemed to please him to sneer, which he could continue to do, even as circumstances showed how wrong he was.

That Johnson's ideas were outside the British mainstream is proved by what happened when the Beatles played Washington, DC. The British Embassy there held a cocktail party to which the Beatles were invited (and no amount of pressure from Epstein and his minions could get them out of it). The result was a mob scene—but not a mob of Beatlemaniacs. The embassy employees, their wives, and their guests behaved as if they were at the zoo. As Beatles biographer Philip Norman sums it up, "Men in stiff collars and their gin-and-tonic wives pushed and struggled for autographs, at the same time exclaiming in patrician amusement, 'Can they actually *write*?'" One of these sophisticated beasts actually cut off a strand of Ringo's hair.

With that, John Lennon began to stride out in anger. He was forbidden to do so.

The embassy staff's condescension was complete. They'd invited the Beatles, it turned out, to pick the winner of a staff raffle—the group was expected to pluck the winning ticket out of a bowl (no doubt a very elegant bowl). Lennon was prepared to challenge whomever he had to in order to get out of this swamp of snobbery. But Ringo put his hand on his mate's shoulder and simply said, "Come on, John. Let's get it over with."

As it developed, to the chagrin of all such snobs, the Beatles got it over with in many senses. (Lennon would eventually even be able to reject the Member of the Order of the British Empire medal that Epstein wouldn't permit him to spurn when it was first awarded.) While it would be a grave error to suppose that such patronizing behavior couldn't (or doesn't) take place 40 years later, at least today the tuxedoed barbarians behave themselves with minimal courtesy, or so it is said.

But in America, Beatlemania represented a different kind of threat. There the fear and loathing of Beatlism and all it represented wasn't confined to the educated and powerful. All sorts of people hated the Beatles, their music, and their loyal audience. In America, records would be burned, it would be proposed that the Beatles be run out of the country (and their long-haired acolytes along with them), and from time to time, fans were indeed punished for liking them. There was nothing "mere" about it, because the American hostility had much deeper origins.

3

TAKING IT TOO SERIOUSLY

In America, rock'n'roll music, and the rhythm and blues and soul music that were part of it, smelled of something more powerful than license and delinquency, poor breeding and lack of education, lower-class status and poverty. It smacked of race.

The proximity of the Beatles' arrival in America and the assassination of President John F. Kennedy two months before (on the very release date of *With the Beatles*) strikes me as mere coincidence. But the arrival of the Beatles necessarily must be connected to the conflagrations and controversy produced by the Southern civil rights movement. The link in this case isn't to an otherwise unrelated point in time, but to the fundamental basis of the music that sparked Beatlemania—something contained within it that has never been expunged.

After World War II, the civil rights movement steadily escalated its assault on the Jim Crow system of legal segregation. Beginning in 1960, students played a leading role, first with the sit-ins in Greensboro, North Carolina, then in 1961 with the Freedom Rides that eventually outlawed segregated interstate travel, but initially made national headlines due to the extremely violent reactions of whites in South Carolina, Alabama, and Mississippi. In 1963, the crisis in Birmingham, Alabama, added a new dimension to the horrific last stand of Jim Crow when police commissioner Bull Connor used water cannons and snarling police dogs to fight off nonviolent protest marchers, many of them of high school age or even younger. On June 12, as the movement began to build toward an assault on segregation's most notorious bastion, Mississippi, state NAACP leader Medgar Evers was murdered in his own driveway. On September 15, the bombing of the Sixteenth Street Baptist Church, Birmingham's movement headquarters, killed four black girls ages 11 and 14—just the age of many Beatles fans, although any black teenage girls screaming lustily for John, Paul, George, and Ringo were kept well out of view of news cameras.

When the Beatles first hit the US airwaves in late December 1963, the Mississippi Summer Project had already begun to recruit college students to participate in a Freedom Summer campaign in which they'd work from June to August 1964 to increase voter registration and civic participation within Mississippi's black communities. On Father's Day weekend in June 1964, Freedom Summer activists James Chaney, Mickey Schwerner, and

Andrew Goodman were found beaten, shot, and buried in a dam in Neshoba County.

That spring and early summer, the Beatles had *Meet the Beatles*, the *Second Album*, and *Introducing the Beatles* all at or near the top of the album charts, a flurry of entries on the singles charts, and *A Hard Day's Night* waiting in the wings ("You Can't Do That" on the *Second Album* came from the film, months early). During this time, in both the South and many urban Northern areas with large black populations, there was daily turmoil. Even if only white kids were Beatles fans—and that was by no means the case—a lot of Beatlemaniacs had both things on their minds.

That's partly because the civil rights movement had an impressive musical culture of its own, with all manner of songs, from century-old spirituals and hymns to adaptations of R&B and rock'n'roll hits with "freedom lyrics" that made specific reference to the current struggle. Many of these came from the Nashville Movement, which was led by students from the city's black colleges, and from the major youth group of the movement, the Student Nonviolent Coordinating Committee (SNCC). There were also original songs, including "topical" songs from the urban folk movement; Bob Dylan's "The Lonesome Death of Hattie Carroll" and "Only a Pawn in Their Game" are good examples.

There were a few overt links between the music of the civil rights movement and the Beatles' music that kindled the British Invasion. For instance, the Beatles recorded (but didn't release at that time) the Little Willie John R&B song "Leave My Kitten Alone," which Nashville students adapted as "You Better Leave My Desegregation Alone."

The Beatles probably knew virtually nothing of such things. But they showed their allegiance to the principles of the civil rights movement when they refused to play any racially segregated shows on their concert tour. It was an unusual statement. The Beatles never again took a political stand as a group, and very few performers made such demands when they worked in the South. Making that choice did not endear them to many white American adults, Southern or Northern.

I never knew about the Beatles refusing to play ball with Jim Crow—or if I did, I had long forgotten it until researching this book. But one reason I've always cherished *The Beatles' Second Album* is that it comes as close to being an R&B album as anything they ever recorded. Not nearly as close as the early records by the Rolling Stones, the Animals, or, for one glorious moment, the Who—records I came to revere, but all of which were over the horizon.

More than half of the *Second Album* originated in rhythm and blues and soul (two different names for similar black vocal music): "Roll Over Beethoven" and "Long Tall Sally," defining moments from the fifties pioneers;

three early hits from newly emergent Motown Records, the Miracles' "You Really Got a Hold On Me," the Marvelettes' "Please Mr. Postman," and Barrett Strong's monumental "Money"; and a very obscure girl-group number, "Devil in Her Heart," which was so far from being a hit that the original version by the Donays didn't make any of the music industry trade-paper charts.

It mattered to me that the Beatles respected such music enough to record it alongside their own when it might have been more profitable to gussy up adult crap like "A Taste of Honey." Maybe you could say that I had become a premature teenage soul snob. But there were things, especially one thing, on *Meet the Beatles* that I mistrusted. The teenage me worried that doing "Till There Was You," a cornball ballad, meant that these guys still might be faking it, willing to sell out the heart in their records for some bogus standard of "musical excellence." "She Loves You" would have remained one of the defining moments of my musical life no matter what, but I wondered, after hearing Paul sing that Meredith Willson rubbish, how much commitment they had to the music that *mattered*.

I knew, or thought I could hear, which music that was—which music was meant to describe the real world, which to conceal it; which music was meant to deceive your heart, which to unleash your dreams; what was sentimental and what was from the soulful depths. If this sounds like I'm claiming that I had already at least an intuition about how important rock'n'roll music might become . . . yeah, that's about right. And the thing I knew, absolutely for certain, was that you could make mistakes but you couldn't fake it because the fakery shone through.

My problem wasn't that "Till There Was You" was a ballad. Ballads were no problem—hell, I loved the ballads of Little Willie John, Sam Cooke, Elvis, and the Shirelles. The Beatles' "This Boy" was no problem at all, because in its cadences and quiet confessions I could hear traces of those performers (particularly the Shirelles; I always thought "This Boy" sounded like a cross between two of their early hits, "Boys" and "Baby It's You," both of which the Beatles recorded).

But "Till There Was You" had no traces of that music; it was straight-up, carefully composed, milk-the-tear-ducts-for-all-they-are-worth-so-the-cash-registers-will-ring show music. This made me suspicious of what these British guys might be up to. A few of their other songs, like "All My Loving" and "P.S. I Love You," already struck me as pretty soft.

For all I knew, the true heart's desire of the Beatles might be to sing "legitimate music," standards, show tunes, or whatever name could be given to what I considered dead-hearted rubbish. I was already deeply infected with my unshakable lifelong prejudice that the only meaningful singing comes in the accents of gospel or blues—although I certainly didn't yet have a name for that style, or any description other than "good" and maybe "sounds right."

I remember looking at the *Second Album* as a kind of

test. If this album contained a bunch of other songs from Meredith Willson or some other guy who didn't know Buddy Holly and Fats Domino from Christmas ornaments, then I could like the Beatles but never love them.

Finding out that they knew what to do with some of the best Motown songs was a delightful revelation, and even better, they did it in their own way, turning Smokey's "Tighter . . . Tighter . . . Tighter" into an affirmation that ranks with "yeah, yeah, yeah" as a quintessentially Beatles hypnotic assent.

I didn't doubt that the Beatles knew the difference between soulful singing and stuff you hang on a tree, but I wanted a sign of their allegiance to what I'd have called rock'n'roll.

The Beatles' Second Album served me as that sign. It's rock'n'roll to the bone and yeah, I know that it has ballads but, like I said, rock'n'roll contains ballads. Rock's not all swagger and rebellion; it's their opposite, too. In fact, I would say that rock'n'roll contains multitudes or else it would have turned into nothing but a fad. And I would have said that, in so many words, in 1964, too.

———

Maybe I took it too seriously from the beginning. If so, I am in perfect company. So did John Lennon. Rock'n'roll for him, as for me, seems to have been both freedom and torment, freedom to do things the world claimed could not be done, torment because of the obstacles to doing them, including the ones you place there yourself.

———

"I mean I like rock & roll, man. I don't like much else," John told Jann Wenner in a 1970 *Rolling Stone* interview. "There's nothing conceptually better than rock & roll. No group, be it Beatles, Dylan or Stones, has ever improved on 'Whole Lotta Shakin'' for my money. . . .

"It was the only thing that could get through to me out of all the things that were happening when I was fifteen. Rock & roll was real. Everything else was unreal. And the thing about rock & roll, good rock & roll, whatever good means, etc., ha-ha, and all *that* shit, is that it's *real*. And realism gets through to you, *despite* yourself. You recognize something in it which is true. . . . "

Mark you, unlike John Lennon, my ambition wasn't to be a musician; I'd wanted to be a writer for as long as I could remember—my mother said that it was all I ever mentioned since I was seven years old. But you couldn't just read, and there wasn't much on TV that interested me, and there was only one TV in our house in Pontiac, Michigan, anyway; only one record player, too, at that point, and it was in the living room with the TV.

But there were transistor radios and when I got one, I began making a musical world in my head out of the sound that poured through the uncomfortable little earplug. I can tell you the first song I heard through that wire: "Johnny Angel," by Shelley Fabares, brand-new on the charts the week I turned 12. It didn't really make the grade, but there *was* something in the wistfulness with which she sang, and in the echo that surrounded her voice.

I'd already been hooked much younger, when my teen-age aunt babysat and we watched *American Bandstand*, and when my mother ordered one of the *Bandstand* anniversary discs that had on it sides by Chuck Berry, Fats Domino, and I don't remember who else. Even when I was seven or eight the music fascinated me, but by the time that radio came into my life—along with all those hormones—it began to fit together. Or I began to piece it together, take your pick.

I didn't listen to words as much as I listened to performances, I didn't listen to instruments as much as I listened to singers. (I did not sing well or play at all. And I was always a frustrated writer, thank you very much, never a frustrated musician. Well, maybe a frustrated singer, whenever a new Miracles record came out.)

I listened intensely, carefully, and as constantly as possible. Was I discriminating? Not by the standards of any intelligentsia that existed then or probably now. I didn't particularly care for separating the strong from the weak, the important from the trivial, *Huckleberry Finn* from *Uncle Scrooge* (don't get me started). What mattered was what reached me, told me more about myself, my world, and the most opaque objects in it, other people and their walled-off hearts. "Louie Louie" or *The Grapes of Wrath*, it's all the same to me.

Almost no one who's written about those first few weeks when the Beatles arrived in our American lives seems to have been anywhere near this engrossed in music already—at least not rock'n'roll. This pretense is maintained even in the very fine Beatles essay by Greil Marcus in the original *Rolling Stone Illustrated History of Rock & Roll*, even though I know for a fact that if you told Greil that entering the Sistine Chapel would forever preclude him from hearing the Chiffons' "One Fine Day," he would after a decorous interval wave Michelangelo good-bye.

You may think that to believe that the Beatles did not spring full-grown from the head of the Muse and straight onto the stage of *The Ed Sullivan Show* marks me as a traitorous type, not at all the kind of man you want telling you about the early Beatles.

But I'm here to tell you that if you know what a great rock and soul music scene existed when the Beatles came and conquered it so quickly, their feat is all that much more impressive.

I will not, in any event, deny my cultural heritage, the foundation that produced, in the year 1963 BB (Before Beatles), these marvels:

"Da Doo Ron Ron," the Crystals

"He's So Fine," the Chiffons

"Louie Louie," the Kingsmen

"Be My Baby," the Ronettes

"Prisoner of Love," James Brown

"On Broadway," the Drifters

"Heat Wave," Martha and the Vandellas

"Surfin' USA," the Beach Boys

"Fingertips—Pt. 2," Little Stevie Wonder

"Donna the Prima Donna," Dion

That's a very partial list that does not include multiple hits by several of the performers, or indispensable records by Sam Cooke, Jackie Wilson, the Shirelles, the Chantays, Lesley Gore, Doris Troy, Jan and Dean, the Tams, the Cookies, the Angels, Gene Pitney, Bobby "Blue" Bland, the Surfaris, the Four Seasons, and the Rocky Fellers.

Acknowledging that, within the rock'n'roll realm, this is great stuff, some of it as great as "She Loves You," doesn't diminish the Beatles' accomplishments, it gives their achievements both proper context and greater depth, it describes the foundation they built on and how far they soared from it.

———

I don't mean to create any sort of idyllic picture. A weird mix of music was coming through those transistors and from the brown plastic tube set, so badly aged that its housing was cracked, that sat on the table in the bedroom my brother and I shared. A lot of it was pop schlock; you could sit through "Danke Schoen," "Hazy Crazy Lazy Days of Summer," and "Go Away Little Girl" 'til your eyelids drooped and your brain froze.

But then "Green Onions" would come on and thaw it with sheer groove, followed by that little Filipino kid from the Rocky Fellers screeching, "Look at Killer Joe go / Dancing with Marie." Twist records were quite excellent, from the Isley Brothers' ranting "Twist and Shout" to Gary Bonds declaring "Doctors agree, so I've been told / Do the twist and you'll never grow old" in "Dear Lady Twist"—which seemed like a good idea at the time. To summarize: I dance, therefore I think.

That tabletop radio, bought at a junk shop for maybe two dollars, played its own role in magnifying the music's mysteries. At certain frequencies or if played very loud, the cracked housing made music blur into pure fuzztone (until you turned it down and banged on it with your fist). I understood very well what John Lennon meant when he said that for him, part of rock'n'roll's early mystique came from Radio Luxembourg's signal, which barely made it to Liverpool across the English Channel and the width of Great Britain. To his ears, the wow and flutter that accompanied records like "Angel Baby" ("fading and blurred with static like coded messages to an occupied country," in the words of Beatles biographer Philip Norman) were part of the rock'n'roll sound.

Anyway, great records weren't all we heard on the

radio. Some kind of weird mix, maybe meant to satisfy everybody, drove the programming of the Detroit stations. If you listened long enough, you could hear Bobby Rydell or Bobby Bland, the Four Seasons or the Four Preps, the Miracles or Henry Mancini, sometimes even John Lee Hooker or Buck Owens, without changing the station. If you listened at night—any time after about eight—you'd likely hear some record you'd never even heard of, and would never hear again. It might be glad-when-it's-over rubbish. It might be a doo-wop masterpiece.

I spent hours scouting around for "that goddamn rock'n'roll music and the nigger trash that goes along with it," to quote my father more or less verbatim. It all fascinated me, from Jerry Butler and Roy Orbison to the Beach Boys and the Temptations, and upstarts like my fellow 14-year-old, Little Stevie Wonder. I loved girl groups (we already called them that) like the Chiffons and the Crystals and the Shirelles, not for their unbridled passion but for the particular ways in which they bridled it. Some of those records—"Da Doo Ron Ron," "He's So Fine," "Soldier Boy"—turned my head so hard my neck about snapped.

On the other hand, I almost never bought records. I had no money to buy them. My parents, who were thirty-something, had a big package of Glen Miller discs, and an album each by Burl Ives, Mitch Miller, and Lawrence Welk, all of which they received as a premium when they bought the stereo console (separation between speakers the width of the unit, a good three feet).

But people generally didn't buy so many records then. In the wake of Elvis, record sales doubled; they doubled again in the wake of two further revolutions, the Beatles-led British Invasion and transistor electronics.

I had a vague idea who Phil Spector was. I took it for granted that everybody in America heard every single Motown issued at least once or twice. My idea of rebellion was slipping the transistor radio under my pillow after lights-out.

On the other hand, the music had given me that idea of rebellion. That's what I was listening for. It was something to build on, in Pontiac or Liverpool.

So if you'd asked me, then and there, to define an enigma wrapped in a mystery encased in a riddle, I could have told you a very great deal about the Jaynetts' "Sally Go 'Round the Roses," a record as scary as watching Stevie Wonder blow a harmonica the size of a loaf of bread 'til it seemed likely his cheeks would explode. If you wanted to know who spoke for me, I'd have told you Brian Wilson of the Beach Boys, whose records I did find ways to buy, because they talked about what I cared about, which was supposed to mean cars and girls, but in fact meant "In My Room" and "Don't Worry Baby," songs about coping with loneliness and mastering fear. I can't say I didn't listen to the words, but what mattered was mostly the emotional timbre, the voices that stuck out alone in a crowd of instruments or huddled in dim corners in tight three- and four-person packs, the guitars and drums that thundered out and shattered brittle silence, the bass lines that promised secret mobility and the depths of truth.

And you had to listen up, because if you heard it once, that was no guarantee you'd ever hear it again.

The prototype of all such experiences in my life was hearing, exactly once, the Donays' "(He's Got the) Devil in His Heart" on the radio. Or at least I think I did, because the minute George started singing it, the fourth track on the first side of the *Second Album*, I recognized it. It was another decade before I heard the original again but there was some sense memory of it back there in '64.

I wish I could explain how that one listen to the Donays happened. It was an almost impossible bit of luck. The record not only wasn't a national hit, it was obscure even in Detroit, where it was made. It probably wasn't played on the radio 25 times in total (at least before people started digging up rare copies after the Beatles' version came out). There probably were something like 500 copies pressed—there was no reason for more, since its commercial life aborted about as quickly as you'd expect from a disc made by four black high school students, a group that had never recorded before and never would again.

Maybe it was one of those records, like "Born to Run"

and "Every Breath You Take," that seems so familiar the first time you hear it, you figure you've heard it somewhere before and forgotten where. "Devil in His Heart" wasn't even the A side, the one that would have been plugged to radio. That was "Bad Boy," which, according to the Donays' Yvonne Allen, "sold quite well in Michigan." Brent Records, based in New York, had picked it up from producer Richard "Popcorn" Wylie, a minor Motown studio mainstay who in August 1962 was just beginning to make his move as an independent. Who would have flipped it and played the B side? In those days, maybe one of the people on the oldies show at WPON, in Pontiac, or the daring Pete Cavanaugh at WTAC in Flint, who played every Who single that flopped across the rest of America. Maybe one of the late-night guys in Detroit. All I know is: I knew it.

The Donays were a prototypical girl group, lead vocalist Allen joined by Michelle Ray and a pair of sisters, Amy and Janice Gwenn. They never toured, although Allen got around more later, when she was a member of the Elgins as Yvonne Vernee-Allen (as Yvonne Vernee, she made some minor records, nonhits, in the sixties). Their obscurity is so great that there is, through 2007, not a single photograph of the Donays anywhere on the World Wide Web.

Allen, at any rate, gave the performance of just about anybody's life on those two sides. On "Bad Boy," she's basically remaking Dee Dee Sharp's recent hit, "Mashed Potato Time," with a slightly shrill intonation atop a Latin beat that's set up mainly by the piano.

On "(He's Got the) Devil in His Heart," you can still hear the influence of Sharp (and perhaps Ronnie Spector of the Ronettes), but on this side the singing is much more distinctive. This time she rides a rhythm that skirts the perimeters of rumba and plays call-and-response with the chorus: They insist he's the devil at heart; she responds, time and again, that "he's an angel sent to me" (it's the same plot as the first season of *Buffy the Vampire Slayer*). The superb guitar playing, which is the instrumental center of the record, sounds like a piece of moonlight work by one or more of Motown's Funk Brothers (whose guitarists were Eddie Willis, Joe Messina, and Robert White). The drumming, on both sides, is almost unmistakably the Funks' Benny Benjamin, and the bass playing seems likely to be James Jamerson—especially since Jamerson and producer Wylie were old friends from Detroit's Northern High School. Aside from some background piano used to reinforce the Latin riffing, that's the record.

Bob Dylan said it best, 45 years after "Devil in His Heart" was made: "The Donays only made one record. You only have to make one if it's this good."

It's not hard to know how he heard it. Since the Beatles recorded it, "Devil in His Heart" has been reissued several times. (A good CD source, because it also has "Bad

Boy," is *Rockin' on Broadway: The Time, Brent, Shad Story*, which traces the history of the company that released the single nationally. The notes contain the quote from Yvonne Allen used here.)

But how the hell did George Harrison find this obscurer-than-obscure single in Liverpool in 1963?

"Black records weren't played on the BBC, I can assure you of that," wrote Rolling Stones manager/producer Andrew Loog Oldham in his book *2Stoned*. "Occasionally you'd hear something on Radio Luxembourg, and then when the pirate stations offshore started up, they played a couple of black records, but not that many, really."

Mostly, the music came to Merseyside by ship, not in the hold but in the duffels of seamen—black American sailors, known locally as Cunard Yanks (Cunard was a major shipping company). Liverpool had about 300 bands in the late fifties and early sixties—rock'n'roll never died out there, either—and the appetite for good new material was ravenous. Only American songs could fill it; the potentially relevant stuff coming out of London was pretty putrid, and there wasn't much of it anyhow. To find Chan Romero's "Hippy Hippy Shake" (later made famous by the Swinging Blue Jeans, a Liverpool band, and also the number with which the Beatles closed their last few sets at the Cavern) was the equivalent of winning a lottery.

A Cunard Yank undoubtedly sold the Donays single to one of the Beatles—it's easy to imagine that it was George, since he was the one who sang it. It wasn't that George, the youngest member of the band, sounded the most like a girl; none of the Beatles made any attempt to sound female when they did a song that originated with a female artist. But maybe George, the most stubborn Beatle, just made the most sense to take the role of the guy who won't give up against all the gossip coming from his mates about his beloved's demonic essence.

The Beatles probably responded at least as intensely to the Donays' backing track as to the vocals. In particular, George grabs hold of that guitar part and makes it his own from the first note of their record. Ringo charges straight into the song at the top, then shifts to a Latin-derived groove that's fascinating, given his reputation at this point as a rock'n'roller and nothing but. (The over-dubbed maracas help a lot, adding a constant busy rustle.) This time, though, he has an extraordinarily mobile bass line to work with—Paul had been studying Motown quite intently, and now he's elaborating his part so heavily that it amounts to a third guitar figure. Add in much cleaner sound and it's almost inarguable that the Beatles have a better track than the Donays—no matter who was working with Popcorn Wylie.

The vocal arrangement creates bigger problems, mainly because Harrison can't conjure what Yvonne Allen can. She's pissed at her friends for slandering the guy; she's not going to even consider that they're right. He's not denying anything, just insisting that she's such a great, uh, kisser that he's willing to operate under whatever set of illusions is required. Listen to the first time he sings "No, *no*"—where Allen is strident in her denial of the accusations, he's obstinate in his denial of the truth.

The argument is different, too, because Allen's not facing much of a challenge from her backing singers, while Harrison from the beginning has to confront classic Lennon–McCartney harmony (reinforced because the arrangement has them initiating the dialogue). He couldn't win this argument if she were right there, wearing a chastity belt.

The strategy—if that's what it was; it could have been just sound dramatic instinct—is perfect. A guy who came across as forcefully as Yvonne Allen would seem like a bully or a fool, or both. But a guy who sounds vulnerable makes the whole story credible, makes it much more of a story, because Harrison's not just responding to base gossip, he's conceding that his advisers may have a point and it doesn't matter because . . . those eyes, those lips. He makes the song into a grand early Beatles statement of purpose, the other side of the coin to "Roll Over Beethoven": "I'll take my chances because romance is so important to me." (A beautiful line with the internal grace of Smokey Robinson's best.) Maybe it even speaks to the way the Beatles worked together: He who cared the most won the day. Either way, it bespoke the romantic teenage heart.

Maybe Yvonne Allen's tragedy was that she sounded

too grown-up. But more likely, it's just that she didn't sound like a dreamy British pop star. However polar their renditions, Allen and Harrison are forever linked, because both poured into "Devil" all the soul at their command.

———

One of the great discrepancies between living through Beatlemania and the way that Beatles history has been recorded is the small role that the rock'n'roll haters play in the annals. As the tale is usually told, it's as if there were a few days, maybe a couple of months, during which general disapproval of the Beatles, individually and as a group, and of the music—theirs, what they drew upon, what they inspired—ran rampant. Then adults quite jovially saw the light and, with the release of "Michelle," all became sweetness and a quick transformation took place to "All You Need Is Love."

That's not how it played out—not in my hometown, and not for anybody I've ever talked to who lived through it. It might not have been so bad to be a Beatle, with fawning minions, Dylan passing out joints, cocktail parties, and groupies providing blowjobs on the quarter hour. But I know from experience that even within the music world, it took years for most devotees of jazz and classical music to admit that rock'n'roll and what it represents constitutes legitimate music. Many have not yet surrendered, if the ignorant reactions to hip-hop are any measure.

What did rock represent? In the music industry, supposedly, the triumph of crude, cheap sounds, lyrical vulgarity, and delinquent behavior. This concept was fostered in the fifties, when Elvis and *Blackboard Jungle* offered visual prototypes, Chuck Berry created lyrical archetypes, and Little Richard, for one, represented a reality too explicitly carnal and polymorphous perverse to allow honest depiction.

All was not well at any point in the sixties, although the identities of the alleged demons and the precise characteristics of their demonic behavior, even of the evil sounds themselves, changed quite a bit. By 1965, you had five London beatniks, a communist Jewish folksinger from New York fronting an insanely loud rock'n'roll band, and four lively lads from Liverpool who in the end refused to humble themselves even before Christ Jesus his own vengeful self.

Nor did the problem confine itself to redneck evangelicals in the Bible Belt and the Deep South.

"The permissive air throughout the 50 states today was not evident 30 years ago in the music business," wrote Capitol Records A&R man Dave Dexter Jr., a jazz sophisticate for almost half a century, in his 1976 autobiography, *Playback*. "America's favorite female singers ... all reflected an innocent, almost virginal, purity in their images ... "

This is nonsense. Dexter describes his favorite female singer of all time, Mildred Bailey, as foulmouthed, obese, and drunken. He also describes his work with Julia Lee, a black R&B singer who "came across on shellac like a bitch in heat," with whom Dexter himself produced such virginal gems as "King Sized Papa," "Snatch and Grab It," and "Gotta Gimme What'cha Got." A photo caption, perhaps written by the author, perhaps not, says "no one found them offensive" (wanna bet?), but of course, in one respect, Dexter was just reflecting white supremacy's conception of white women's stature versus that of black women.

It's not even that Dexter "knew better." He didn't just recite the standard cant on why music—the whole of popular culture really, even the part that turned out Annette Funicello and Shelley Fabares, I suppose—had become immoral. He believed it, felt it placed his own Beatles-adoring children in mortal jeopardy. And this is a guy who made a set of (pretty great) records with a twice-convicted murderer—Leadbelly.

When the rock haters turned from morals to music, the comments were nastier, more self-contradictory, and not so much ignorant as deeply, willfully stupid, flying in the face of sociology, psychology, and musicology, generally without the remotest inkling that there was more than one way in which to make important music. Dexter makes a distinction between rock'n'roll and what he calls "legitimate music." He never defines the difference, but even that late in the rock'n'roll wars, he wouldn't have needed to. Five years after Dexter published *Playback*, when my brother told my father that he thought this rock-writing thing looked like it would work out for me since I had placed a book on the best-seller list, he says my dad replied, "Rick! Don't you know that this rock'n'roll thing is just a fad?"

The jaundiced snobbery and proud ignorance of such comments represent the loads of such codswallop rock fans—and later, as rap replaced rock at the center of popular music culture, hip-hop fans—have endured for half a century, with a new crusade to return us to the "almost virginal purity" of "King Sized Papa" and, for that matter, the jaded cokehead lyrics of "I Get a Kick Out of You."

I am not reciting ancient, empty history: In 2004, a school superintendent in Benton Harbor, Michigan, banned the high school band from playing "Louie Louie" because of the song's "immoral lyrics." This was done by a black superintendent, to protect kids from a song even the FBI eventually recognized has no dirty lyrics, and by the way, the band would have played a version of the song with no singing.

Now, imagine taking mandatory music classes in Pontiac, Michigan, in early 1964, with "Louie Louie" still on the radio, the Beatles everywhere, Motown erupting in the near distance, and the entire city government fighting to preserve its functionally segregated school system.

Music was a required course through ninth grade. (This was back before America chose to believe itself too poor to sponsor such frills as music, art, even athletics in the public schools.) What they were supposedly teaching us, I cannot imagine. We didn't have instruments; that was a separate class. We didn't learn to read music. We barely learned anything about singing, and even in terms of music history, we barely got names or dates or great composers.

But I think the curriculum or the motivation behind the curriculum is not so hard to discern. The only time anyone ever dealt out corporal punishment to me was in a music class, in about third grade, when I became so absorbed in some song we were singing—a folk song, "Erie Canal," suggests itself as my accomplice—that I tranced out, as still happens when a song or story particularly fascinates me. The grim-faced music teacher, a humorless wretch who reminded me of the Wicked Witch of the West minus anything so amusing as that cackle, gave me several whacks with a yardstick. It was more humiliating than painful, which was, of course, the idea. The lesson I took from this was that what was really being taught in those classes was discipline and conformity, a situation that fit me like a burlap sack with manacles.

The Wicked Witch of LeBaron Elementary sniffed periodically about the stupidity and inferiority of the music we liked. But she was nothing next to the guy who taught music at Madison Junior High.

His name I mercifully do not recall, probably because he never smacked me around. He looked like somebody who'd have worked as an under-assistant to Willy Loman, rotund, white shirt, black tie, a nebbish, cocksure only in his ability to hector teenagers about the errors of their ears. He made making music seem about as appealing as having your eardrums pierced; he made listening to it a chore duller than conjugating Latin verbs. He seemed to subscribe to the worst fallacy in education, the idea that knowledge of a particular set of rules gave him the privilege of ignoring or making sport of all that lay outside them. He made little effort to communicate what was important about the kind of music he liked—he presented the rules and some assertions, that was all.

We had music class a couple of days a week. I'd say about every third class, before and during (there is no after) the Beatlemania spasm, The Music Teacher would rise up in dudgeon amidst the 20 or so newly minted teenagers under his gaze to harangue us with epithets about Beatlism, Motown, and this rock'n'roll stuff in general. It was like an obsession with him, although I suspect it was also school policy, or maybe the quintessence of current educational theory in the field: Batter the little asswipes 'til they surrender.

I knew of no administrator, colleague, or parent who'd have disagreed with The Music Teacher's values and methodology. At least no one who'd demur in public. But if I got home from school a little early, my mother had likely set up the ironing board in front of the TV set so she could watch *American Bandstand*. My father, though, made the school officials look positively empathetic. The Music Teacher did an hour or so once a week on the topic; my dad sometimes did twice that much every night for a week.

This endless harping stemmed not from the music but from the whole package: the longish hair, the unusual clothing (particular offense was taken to the footwear, which around our parts translated to Cuban-heeled boots of either black leather or suede), and the general attitude that the Beatles gave of being saturated in that greatest of all terrors, freedom. Freedom from conformity, freedom from the imposition of time-honored standards (that is, mores that were maybe 50 years old), freedom from dealing with life and its accoutrements without irony, freedom from knowing one's place in the world, freedom to make a new place.

If you live in a company town—which is what Pontiac was, though by then we were all well on our way to living in a company world—freedom is a dangerous thing. Without the kind of freedom the Beatles represented, material comfort of all sorts was possible, even job security (many supposed). With such freedom, there would be nothing but trouble.

The Beatles were hated, as much as anything, for representing the principle that freedom was worse than available. It was fun.

The Beatles were an infection carrying a double virus—on the one hand, this freedom thing, and on the other, the plague of blackness, a term that is, of course, about 200 percent too polite compared to what was actually said. The beat was both things—free and black. It was, as the teacher implied and my father and his cronies told us explicitly, a fool's paradise, a nigger heaven, for which we reached.

If this sounds like a teenager's overreaction, or just plain confused, maybe it was some of both those things. It was as if there was a code among the schoolteachers that everybody understood, without ever admitting that it was understood, the white working-class equivalent of the phenomenon of "double consciousness"—living with knowledge of two fundamental facts about one's self, neither quite false or quite true—that W. E. B. DuBois describes in *The Souls of Black Folk.* I don't know what was in that teacher's conscious mind; I do know that everything he tried to teach us smacked of the message I got at home, which was that white was right and black needed to be kept back, or, since it was advancing, north and south, into territory that had been "ours," pushed back.

That stuff about the Beatles being revolutionary is more than just talk. There was a war going on, and we were asked to take sides.

———

I don't know how many rock bands the Beatles spawned. There might have been, at one point or another between '64 and '68, 1,000 in Detroit alone. There might have been 10,000 across the United States, and the number might go into six figures if you counted other places (Mexico, Indonesia, the Philippines, Brazil) where the impact of the British Invasion spurred many to try to do it themselves—not just to listen, but to play and sing.

It was the same everywhere, and it was different everywhere. As David Reyes and Tom Waldman write in *Land of a Thousand Dances: Chicano Rock 'n' Roll from Southern California*, "Seemingly every high school kid and many junior high school kids in that part of the city wanted to form a band, if only for the camaraderie and the sheer joy of playing. The groups all dressed in suits, á la the Beatles, and they invented wonderful band names such as Thee Epics, the Ambertones, the Heartbreakers, Thee Righteous Rhythms, the Apollos. As much as the music, the names and the audience constituted the swagger of Chicano rock 'n' roll in the mid-sixties." That was one version; the power pop of the Northeast (Barry and the Remains) was another; the maniac proto-punk thump of the Pacific Northwest (the Sonics) was a third; the acoustic bohemian community's folk rock (the Byrds) was a fourth.

In Detroit, the idea had already been brought home by earlier groups, most notably Mitch Ryder and the Detroit Wheels. Mitch and his band, then still called Billy Lee and the Rivieras, threw down a tough challenge because they had taken the R&B and soul music on which everything was built and turned it into a sound of their own, careening through a medley, "Jenny Take a Ride," that fused Little Richard's "Jenny, Jenny" with the antique-blues "C.C. Rider," which traced back beyond Ma Rainey but didn't seem so antique once Chuck Willis reinvented it in 1957 by adapting the beat to fit the line dance called the stroll.

There were other white groups that could "sound black," too. There was, for one, the Four Seasons, who managed to capture the keening high tenor and falsetto leads of doo-wop as they merged into early soul on records like "Sherry." Billy Lee and the boys hadn't made their first record yet in 1964, but they were local legends. The Seasons had already been on the charts so long that by February 1964, they were on their fifth top-10 hit, "Dawn." From time to time, the Beach Boys could hit that mark, too, especially with the Chuck Berry licks in "Shut Down" and "Fun, Fun, Fun" (which also hit the charts that February, along with its B side, a remake of Frankie Lymon's doo-wop masterpiece, "Why Do Fools Fall in Love").

The point wasn't really that these guys sounded black. I can't remember thinking that Frankie Valli of the Four Seasons might be a black singer, even though he was in effect the white Frank Lymon. I can't even remember thinking it about Mitch Ryder, who was assuredly the white Wilson Pickett. That wasn't the point. The point was that they used the same materials to sound so impermissibly like themselves.

This was the standard some of us wanted the Beatles to

reach. We weren't content to hear the folk chords that rushed by in "I Want to Hold Your Hand." We wanted a shot of rhythm and blues, a bigger shot than *Meet the Beatles* gave us. We wanted it for the danger, for the commitment, for the sound, for the feeling that if there was a revolution going on, it went all the way to the core.

The Beatles' Second Album delivered on every bit of that promise. Paul McCartney's never sounded more like a dedicated rocker than on his balls-out romp through "Long Tall Sally," which was not so much about sex as it *was* sex. (When Pat Boone tried to steal Little Richard's first hit, "Tutti Frutti," he sounded like he was reciting a text from an alien culture; when he tried to steal "Sally," Richard's second smash, Boone sounded like he belonged to an alien species, one that reproduced by parthenogenesis.)

Richard probably had the purest voice of any rocker of the first generation bar Sam Cooke, and McCartney's absolute devotion to his style comes across with undiluted potency, a little hint of what the Beatles had learned while playing for all those months in bars in the whorehouse district of Hamburg. McCartney approaches the key lyric—"We're gonna have some fun tonight / Everything's all right"—with just as much subtlety as Richard, which was none. You could say he erased any hint of decorum but what he, like his idol, really smashed was pretense and euphemism. To me, living in a place where it seemed like a main lesson to learn was that "fun" was a dirty word, it made perfect sense, and the Beatles played it with a rush of joy that said they thought the same.

Now it's true that Paul does not hit the high notes with as much gospel power as Richard, it's true that he does not sound cunning in the way that Richard, in the midst of his mania, always did. It doesn't matter much. It doesn't even matter that Paul had already shown his Little Richard moves to brilliant effect on "I Saw Her Standing There."

The story of the song is the passion with which Paul pulls you into it, his complete conviction that he can put the song across as himself, not a rock-star manqué but the authentic article. "Long Tall Sally" isn't an homage like "Roll Over Beethoven," it's personal expression, the art of rock'n'roll at a very high level.

The original "Long Tall Sally" is piano music, but on Richard's original, the instrumental break is dominated by Lee Allen's sax and Earl Palmer's drums playing an apotheosis of the New Orleans shuffle. Richard gives a singularly stentorian, almost hoarse, shouting vocal, a little ragged but exactly right. "Long Tall Sally" is one of the documents that established the art of rock'n'roll.

Little Richard met the Beatles in London in 1962, just as their star was beginning to rise. He was making something of a comeback after his legendary retirement to join the Christian ministry. He played New Brighton Tower in Liverpool, and Brian Epstein arranged another concert for him at Liverpool's Empire Theater, on October 28,

1962, with the Beatles as the opening act. Richard, whose tales are wild and frighteningly often verifiable, claims to have somewhere in this period given Paul McCartney a screaming lesson. (He unquestionably gave the band a career-long sideman, his keyboard player and singer Billy Preston. Richard abandoned Preston in England, and the Beatles helped him find refuge. Later, Billy had a hit on the Beatles' label, Apple, the pop gospel "That's the Way God Planned It.")

The Beatles play the song like life itself (not just their lives) depends on it. Paul starts at a peak above Richard's normal wild search for ecstasy—McCartney's already found his, and he's celebrating it, not sneaking around in any back alley, but bringing the alley out front. As Tim Riley, one of the few to write about the Beatles' actual music of this period, put it, "He's not interested in explaining his hysteria; and if you have to ask what all the excitement is about, you'll never understand."

At the break, the guitars take charge, competing against Ringo's *ka-boom* and George Martin's insistently clang-ing piano. Martin does add a swooping glissando (á la Jerry Lee Lewis) toward the end of this section. It's a setup for McCartney's return, with a "woooo" that is not Richard's because it's a sound of his own. His "waaaaah!" comes from some other place altogether; he sounds like he's been goosed by the gods. And that last ringing chord—that's the siren call for those 100,000 rock bands the Beatles had already inspired.

The whole thing is one indomitable, unforgettable take. It's probably as close to Hamburg and the Liverpool of the Cavern Club after Hamburg as they ever got in the studio. It's certainly as close as Lennon's legendary one-take "Twist and Shout." This is a great rock'n'roll band at the peak of its form, and a firm and final rebuttal of the canard that Paul McCartney is not a great rock'n'roll singer—there's rarely been a better one.

The Beatles knew they had command of the song and, with it, a stake all the way back to the dawn of rock history, too, for in its different way, "Long Tall Sally," with its leering comments about having some fun tonight, was as much an anthem as "Roll Over Beethoven." They closed shows with "Long Tall Sally" all through 1964 and revived it at the end of their San Francisco Cow Palace show in 1966, the last song of the last live concert they ever did together. (It is the one song from the show that, so far as we know, does not exist on tape.) They did the song on British television, and seven times played it live for BBC Radio broadcasts. It wouldn't be surprising if more people think it's their song than know it's Little Richard's. And while, as it happens, Little Richard is one my rock'n'roll idols, I think that's perfectly understandable, even acceptable, their reward for a dead heat in the race for quality.

4

THE SOUND OF YOUNG BRITANNIA

Liverpool and Detroit have a lot in common.

You figured I'd say that. But they do. For one thing, they are two of the very few places where the idea of the rock band survived the fifties. For another, they were, at the peak of their existence, cities where the technological arc of their time crossed with its economic arc and produced untold riches, and left misery in its wake. In Detroit, it was all cars, until it wasn't; the richest working-class community in the world was reduced to literal rubble in a decade. In Liverpool in the 18th century, because of Britain's fleet of ultramodern sailing ships, the slave trade from Africa crossed with the cotton trade from North America. The one cargo was forbidden to land in England on its way west, the other was entirely uncrated there and packed off to the manufacturing cities further east in the Midlands (Manchester, Birmingham) on one of the first important railroad lines in the world.

For a third, Liverpool and Detroit were places where lines of race and class went underground, hid beneath the surface, and then boiled upward. The British slave trade ended in 1807, after decades of exhaustive debate in Parliament. During that time, Liverpool merchants got up more than 50 petitions against abolition—not in favor of restoring British slavery but in favor of continuing the buying and selling of slaves, the reduction of human beings into property, the reduction of life into mere machinery. The city's dockyards and the Cotton Exchange (where Jim McCartney, Paul's father, worked) attracted a second group of the despised, Irish immigrants from just across the Channel, who began to arrive when it was still illegal to practice their religion in England and kept coming because there was money to be made—not riches, but a living, which was more than could be said for Ireland. There were 80,000 Irish in Liverpool in 1800, 160,000 in 1820. To characterize the Irish as despised puts it very mildly.

Detroit saw immigration from all over the globe. In 1964, the area contained communities of Maltese, Palestinians, Greek Cypriots, and Lebanese that were the largest in the world outside their native countries. From the 1920s into the 1950s, a huge migration of blacks from the southern United States took place. The first "troubles" involving race began in 1925, the city nearly burned to the ground in the race riot of 1943, and in 1967, substantial parts of it did burn down and were never rebuilt.

In both Detroit and Liverpool, tension and despair were constants, but so was a culture of joy. Detroit has produced an outsize number of musicians, particularly jazz, rhythm and blues, and rock musicians. In addition to its remarkable number of rock musicians and comedians, Liverpool also has produced a significant number of playwrights, actors, and other performers.

John Lennon understood this well. "Because it was a port, that means it was less hick than somewhere in the Midlands," he told Jann Wenner in *Lennon Remembers.* "We were a port, the second biggest port in England. Also between Manchester and Liverpool, the North was where all the money was made in the 1800s or whenever it was, that was where all the brass and the heavy people were. And that's where the despised people were. We were the ones that were looked down upon by the southerners as *animals.* . . . It was a very poor city and tough. But people had a sense of humor, because they're in so much pain. So they're always cracking jokes, they're very witty. And it's an Irish place. It's where the Irish came when they ran out of potatoes. And it's where black people were left or worked as slaves or whatever, and the trader communities. It's cosmopolitan, and it's where the sailors would come home with the black records from America on the ships!"

This helps explain why the Beatles, before any other white rock performers in England or anywhere else, became Motown fans and, more important, Motown emulators.

I don't mean Motown imitators. The Beatles never did anything half so crude as ape another style. They personalized every bit of music they touched, and the records they made of Motown hits, which are gathered in a bundle on the *Second Album*, prove it as much as any records they ever made. As Tim Riley wrote, "What they learned from the records they copied was not merely how to sound like someone else, but how to play and sing, how to put a song forward. 'Don't copy the swimming teacher, learn how to swim'" is how John Lennon put it.

By the time they began recording for EMI with George Martin, they were past copying. They and Martin bothered only with arrangements and performances that transcended or at least aimed to transcend the originals. Mostly they got there, and to get there with Motown material like "You Really Got a Hold On Me," "Please Mr. Postman," and, particularly, "Money" was especially impressive, because Motown was the cutting edge of American soul music, the kind of thing that most white groups and singers shied away from altogether because it was just too tough to come close to the quality of the originals. (To my ear, the Rolling Stones' early efforts at Motown are pallid, and while I like the Who doing "Heatwave," all that shows is that I'm a terminal Who fan.)

The Motown songs the Beatles chose were all huge

hits, very well known to R&B fans in the United States and much more well known than most Motown records could have been in England. On the other hand, "Please Mr. Postman" by the Marvelettes, although Motown's first number-one pop hit in 1963, required a gender spin similar to that given to "Devil in His Heart." Barrett Strong's 1960 "Money," although it was the first national hit for Berry Gordy's fledgling label, only reached number 29 on the American pop singles chart (and Strong never had another chart hit), so it was not all that well known even in the States. The Miracles' "You Really Got a Hold On Me," though, made it to number one on the R&B chart and number eight on the pop chart, and was perhaps the defining moment for songwriter and lead vocalist Smokey Robinson and his group. But it was not the kind of iconic hit that "Roll Over Beethoven" and "Long Tall Sally" were.

Nevertheless, the fact that the Motown records were contemporary—the Miracles put "You Really Got a Hold On Me" on the American charts in November 1962, smack between the UK success of the Beatles' "Love Me Do" and "Please Please Me"—created some additional risks in remaking them. These songs were much more certain to be familiar to American audiences than the fifties numbers they did, and therefore, fans could make comparisons between them much more directly. Also, the Motown band set a very high standard because it played more sophisticated music than the rock'n'roll bands of

Berry and Richard, especially the bass lines of James Jamerson and the drumming of Benny Benjamin. (It was a feat for the Beatles to come as close to the Funk Brothers as they did on "Devil in Her Heart," let alone coming up against some of the Funks' best-known material.)

The Motown songs weren't anthems. "Money" was a slightly dour look at avarice interacting with emotion; "Please Mr. Postman" was both a dance record, its beat perfect for the twist, the craze of 1961, and a sweet girl-group lament for a lost lover; "You Really Got a Hold On Me" was a kind of soul-style torch song, Smokey Robinson's high tenor conveying both mad passion and yearning for more than that against his group's smooth, post-doo-wop harmony. Finding your way into these songs was not simply a matter of liking them or drumming up a similar enthusiasm or having them speak for you by their nature, which is how "Beethoven" and "Sally" worked.

The Beatles ceased recording material from outside the group within a few months after the *Second Album*, while Motown began recording Beatles songs during the height of Beatlemania: The Supremes, the Temptations, Martha and the Vandellas, and others all made Beatles tracks, but only Stevie Wonder's "We Can Work It Out," a hit in 1971, proved worthwhile. Be that as it may, there is a spiritual affinity between the Beatles, particularly as writers and record makers, and the main Motown producer/songwriters, Holland–Dozier–Holland and Smokey

Robinson. Robinson and Eddie Holland, although it is rarely noted, probably come closer than any other major songwriters of the period, certainly much closer than Bob Dylan or the Rolling Stones, to having a lyrical sensibility similar to Lennon and McCartney's (if you skip over John and Paul's psychedelic period—which is not the worst idea).

"Please Mr. Postman" is a Holland–Dozier–Holland production, but only Brian Holland had a hand in writing the song. Marvin Gaye plays drums on the original by the Marvelettes (a trio from all-black Inkster, Michigan), and it's a great part, with a fatback turnaround that makes it more a dance record than a girl-group hit. Gladys Horton's lead vocal is gritty almost to a fault, and her delivery of the climactic line, "Delivah de lettah / De soonah de bettah," ranks among Motown's most fabulous moments.

Such stuff always grabbed John Lennon's attention, but what in the world tempted him to try singing the song? Maybe the intricate timing. Much of the record alternates between drawn-out vowels followed by staccato syllabic breakdown ("Soooo paaaaa-tient-ly" takes up an entire line in the third verse; the line before it has 12 syllables, yet somehow the two come out exactly right, just like the eight syllable lines in all the other verses.) Some of it must have been that funky beat. Or maybe he just wanted to hear himself sing that "deliv-ah de lett-ah" line.

Horton is pretty cool, for a woman in despair over the silence of her lover. The other Marvelettes sing like they're just passersby wanting to help out the lady with the problem—they've seen it before, they've been this woman, their job now is just to get the mailman's attention, snapping "Wait!" and adding "oh yeah" to her every plea and explanation, the girl-group equivalent of shouting "amen" and "hallelujah." (Some believe that "Postman" is the source of the Beatles' fixation on "yeah" as interjection, rhythmic counterpoint, and all-purpose high-energy signifier on "She Loves You," "It Won't Be Long," and "I'll Get You"—since the first and last of these are on this record, there are probably more iterations of "yeah" on *The Beatles' Second Album* than on any other record ever pressed.)

However much the Beatles, and Lennon in particular, loved the Marvelettes' record, it did not prevent them from aiming to destroy its quotient of reserve. The Beatles' "Postman" amounts to a garage-punk assault on R&B, laying beat and melody to waste in search of sheer sonic excitement; it's a kick, it's thrilling . . . but wait, isn't that John Lennon there, insisting that the agony is just as real for all of that?

There's a groove to it, Ringo's clipped cymbal splash, then John's shattering "Wait! . . . Oh yes, Mr. Postman"—*yes*, not *yeah!* like the proper Englishman he was raised to be. At the beginning his various pleadings are almost too coherent. But soon you realize that it's Paul and George's "harmony" vocals that tell the story while Ringo eggs all three of them on.

When John takes it over, there's a sob in his throat and a gleam in his eye that flies right past anything Gladys Horton sounds like she imagined. He wants the letter; he wants the girl, but mainly . . . he wants.

My music classes were such an awful experience that I am pretty sure that every guy in school thought singing was a sissy sport. But John's playing football, tackle, no pads. "Check it and see, one more time for me!" It's a plea, a demand, a last resort, all he knows and way beyond anything he understands—it's all feeling, summoning a hero's actions while denying heroism (since there's nothing he can do to make that letter arrive but . . . Wait!). This is *nothing* sissy, or if it is, then sissy's all right.

He hits "so-oo-oh pa-tient-ly" beautifully, but where you can feel his heart being rent is every time the song lets him breathe "oooohhh yeah."

"You didn't stop to make me feel better . . . " The scene is so primordial, so physical, so rejected and revolted, and in love and stunned and bemused and terrified that I imagine 17-year-old John on the corner of Menlove Avenue, watching his beloved Julia—mother, muse, nemesis—as she's hit by the car. (He did not see that happen in reality. But he sings like the screech of the tires still haunts his ears.)

Then he's back to being the teenage goof-off: "Delivuh de lettuh, de soonah de bettuh" like he's channeling

Jughead and Maynard G. Krebs, jetting out of the corner he's painted himself into. Tough guy with a tear in his eye, or at least his larynx. There's no way off that corner or out of it, either.

You don't think that's a liberation, a way of serving notice that you can be all you can be? You've forgotten what it is to be a teenager.

John Lennon never did, and he inspired a generation to remember with him.

———

"You Really Got a Hold On Me" has a magical place in my life. One Sunday evening, around the time the Beatles showed up, I was laying in my top bunk bed listening to the weekly oldies show on WPON. The disc jockey played the Miracles singing that song. The record lasted the length of time it always does—a few seconds shy of three minutes—but that night, it was over in a second that amounted to a lifetime.

I had seen the Miracles somewhere and I knew that Smokey and his group were black. In that lifetime's second, as the tight, slow drag groove hammered at my nerves, the piano insistent as a bad conscience, Smokey's lead voice like my own cracked mind, I knew one thing for damned sure: There was nothing inferior about these people, and if that was true, nothing else I'd been told about why white was supreme possibly could be. I can remember climbing down from that bed and walking into the next room, feeling like an explorer. Every drumbeat, every sax riff, and every quaver in Smokey's beautiful vocal is imprinted on my mind, or in my bloodstream, or signed with a knife across my heart. To this day. And I thank him for it, pretty much every day.

Trying now to listen with new ears, I hear sadness, a man fighting his own desires, a guy trying to work out his next hit, his relations with the people around him (great drummer, unbelievable singers including his wife, Claudette, and then there's the monomaniac at the piano—Berry Gordy maybe or my one-time drinking companion, Joe Hunter), a guy who's worried about whether he can get through the tricky parts ("Hold me . . . please, hold me . . . squeeze"), nothing in his mind at all about changing any lives except those he can touch and see.

I know exactly why I heard the record so clearly. I love that voice, it's the voice I would have if you got to pick your voice, it's vulnerable and calculating, it's smart and it's injured, it's in search of justice ("You do me wrong now / My love is strong now"), it's a man in love with beauty and the beat. When he sings "Tighter" (just twice, the second time doubled by Claudette) he's commanding the musical universe, just for those three minutes, no longer, no longer is necessary.

But it's not the voice I have, not the singing voice or the mental voice. I do not have a singing voice of any consequence (to say the least). My inner voice, the voice of my mind speaking my heart—I can find that directly in John

Lennon's version of "You Really Got a Hold On Me." When he sings, what registers is "I wanna split now . . . I just can't quit now." I don't even remember those words from the Miracles' version (but they're there). As rock historian Charlie Gillett, not generally a devotee of British Invasion R&B, wrote in *The Sound of the City*, Lennon's passion "transformed the innocence of the interpretation by the Miracles . . . into a much stronger song and created a sense of greater resilience behind the tender messages."

There's a choirboy's voice in the cheeky, curmudgeonly young Lennon, and on certain words here, the choirboy is in full control. They aren't big words; they aren't "pataphysical." Just words like "I love you madly" and the "hold" that follows it, and the "hold" that follows Paul and George's next refrain, "my love is strong now" like he's running out of breath, and right after that, the "hold" quivering in his throat like a hound dog's yowl, and every time he intones "Baby" and "Tighter" (the capitalization present in his tone). The way he drops his voice into "I just can't quit now."

When Ringo crashes his drums this time, it's like the beat tumbling down a flight of stairs the size of the Spanish Steps. Paul and George's harmonies are perfect, especially the way they join John with overlapping cries of "Baby!" just before the gospel-like explosion near the end. George's guitar has a big, hollow-body tone, Paul's bass stalks the beat, and George Martin feels like a member of the band on piano, stating the melody at the start and then falling back to add weight to the guitar licks. It's a band performance. But that's because it takes a band to support everything John gives.

On the clock, the Beatles' version of "You Really Got a Hold On Me" lasts just a few seconds more than three minutes. It lasts a lifetime in the head.

———

These are great performances. But none of them is the greatest Beatles rendition of a song written and first performed by someone not in the group (so-called "cover songs"). For one thing, none is as outright crazed as "Twist and Shout," which John famously did in a single take with his throat bleeding at the end of a very long session.

In terms of sheer power and rude eloquence, though, Lennon outstripped even "Twist and Shout" with his vocal on "Money (That's What I Want)." In fact, his singing here is as naked, abrasive, honest-to-a-fault, and revealing as anything on his first solo album, *Plastic Ono Band*. He never did better than this, because, as with "She Loves You," there isn't better to do.

Forget the original. Barrett Strong has no lack of desire, but really, he's out on a lark. He's broke, he'd trade his girlfriend—and probably has traded a good part of his self-esteem—for the rent, but he isn't losing sleep over it. He's bound and determined, even driven by the piano that's in charge of the beat (or the tambourine that's in charge of the piano), but he's not haunted. It's a great little record because he keeps his spirit free in the face of the main problem that confronts us all (those who disagree, rattle your jewelry).

A competent version of the Beatles playing "Money" exists on the demos they made during their Decca Records audition on New Year's morning, 1962. The Beatles had driven almost all the snowy night in a freezing van, arrived in the midst of the annual revel around Lord Nelson's statue in Trafalgar Square, and went to bed without supper in a cheap, damp hotel near Decca's West Hampstead studios. They arose the morning of the audition and trudged to the studio by 10 a.m. Mike Smith, the A&R man who ran the demo session, had to fight his own way into town through the snowstorm and arrived an hour late. Add in Pete Best's thud-dud drumming, and their competence perhaps pays tribute to how great three of the Beatles had already become.

The version of "Money" the Beatles recorded on July 18, 1963, has a much more commanding tenor from the moment George Martin's overdubbed piano kicks it off. The piano part is bass heavy and there's still a metallic guitar band feel left over from George's grinding opening riff. Ringo's drumming rides the beat effortlessly. But the music provides mere commentary on the singing. Even during the bridge ("middle eight" to Anglophiles), all you really want is to go back to hearing Paul and George's nagging "That'ssss . . . what I want" chorus that seems meant to provoke Lennon into becoming a relentless raver.

If goading John is what they were up to, it worked. You can take John's singing to be sarcastic, ironic, obsessed, driven, self-reflective, taking it out on the world of mammon, embarrassed by his own riches, greedy for more, lustful in every sense, or repulsed in a whole bunch of ways. I take it to be each of these, not in turn but all at once. That's why the dense, thunderous music feels so right. There's desperation in Paul and George's voices, too, as if they're concerned that Lennon will crash and burn before he finishes.

Indeed, as the lead-in to the bridge, he utters a wail— "Whhhhhaaaaaahhhhh"—that evokes the bleeding yelps of "Twist and Shout." And when he sings, "Whoa, yeah, I wanna be free!" you can throw every descriptive term above into the trash. After that, he rips through the lyric to arrive at what he flat-out means to do with his life— which is not worry about money. That is, he rips up the song and rejects its overt meaning, turns what seems amusingly truthful in Strong's version on its head, so that what Janie Bradford's lyric denies—"What it don't get, I can't use"—becomes the truth he asserts. With the final "That's what I want," John Lennon achieves a singing voice that exactly models his speaking voice, as if to say, "I know how you get free. Sing like this. Become what is in this music."

It's ridiculous, but that's how I have always heard it, and not just because you had to be where I was. Unless by "where I was" you mean listening to John Lennon sing "Money." If Lennon, above any other Beatle, represented the heart of rock and soul music, became its heroic champion rather than just another teenage idol, that moment when he screams "I wanna be free" is the moment when he began to unveil the totality of what he had in mind.

George Martin had exactly the right idea. He sequenced *With the Beatles* so that "Money," with its unanswerable assault on expectations and, for that matter, the reality of conventional contemporary life, ends the show. What could follow this display?

On the *Second Album*, it shows up as the fifth song on the first side, followed by "You Can't Do That," as if to deliberately contradict its meaning.

Hey, I said this was a great album, not a perfect one.

5

LIVERPOOL TO HOLLYWOOD
VIA GARY, INDIANA

The full economic impact of the Beatles on the music industry has never been measured. But they fostered a huge group of changes. They damaged or destroyed the careers of dozens of American performers, made possible or escalated the careers of nearly as many British performers, disrupted or ended the careers of professional songwriters and the businesses of the major US and UK music publishers, and accelerated the careers of many aspiring songwriters, especially those who also performed and fronted bands using electric instruments. They made rock'n'roll a worldwide phenomenon for the first time, for both creators and consumers, in the process pushing all but the most established performers to the margins or out of business entirely and opening the way for rock music in parts of the world where the concept hadn't previously existed.

These changes all took place within the record industry and the songwriting world. The Beatles didn't have nearly as much impact upon the live music industry, but in addition to spawning the bands that would make that impact, they also helped inspire their earliest American booking agent, Frank Barsalona, to create Premier Talent, the first agency that represented only rock music.

In addition to playing a large if not decisive role in putting the great independent rhythm and blues record label, Vee-Jay, out of business, the Beatles affected other record companies. EMI was already the largest record company in the world, but its wholly owned American subsidiary, Capitol, went from also-ran to fully competitive with the giants, CBS and RCA. (America at that time was by far the world's largest market for recorded music, representing as much as half of all world trade in records and tapes.)

Capitol didn't come along willingly. Its international A&R representative, Dave Dexter Jr., rejected the first two Beatles singles so acerbically that he wasn't even offered the third, then he rejected the fourth and tried to reject the fifth before orders from headquarters finally forced his bosses to buy a Beatles single from EMI, the company that owned Capitol. Those singles were "Love Me Do" backed with "P.S. I Love You," "Please Please Me" backed with "Ask Me Why," "From Me to You" backed with "Thank You Girl," "She Loves You" backed with "I'll Get You," and, most stupefying of all, "I Want to Hold Your Hand" backed with "This Boy." Dexter had the same response to all of them: They had no commercial potential in the American market.

Far from being punished for this utter misfeasance (or deafness), Dexter remained the A&R man responsible for each of the band's American releases, including the makeup of their LPs, well into 1966. And even then his role in the story wasn't over.

Dexter played a role almost as hefty as it is hard to believe, but just making him the heavy won't do. To begin with, the full story is much more complicated and interesting. After all, Dexter didn't appoint himself sole arbiter of the Beatles' records. You can't really understand how he was able to do what he did, why he was encouraged to do it, and the consequences—economic and artistic—without understanding more about the world he operated in.

———

Songwriter Johnny Mercer, record store owner Glenn Wallichs, and movie producer Buddy DeSylva started Capitol Records in 1942, a most unpropitious time because World War II was placing severe constraints on the availability of shellac, from which records were then made. The company prevailed because Mercer was a musical genius, Wallichs was a very savvy businessman, and DeSylva had enough sense to stay out of stuff he didn't understand. Capitol was the first record company to see radio as a marketing center rather than a competitor, so it became the first to send disc jockeys free copies of its new releases. In 1948, it became the first to record with magnetic tape, which offered improved opportunities for editing as well as superior fidelity. In the early 1950s, it became the first company to issue records in all current formats—the 78-rpm discs that had been standard since the 1920s, the 33⅓-rpm LPs developed by CBS, and the 45-rpm singles developed by RCA.

Capitol developed extraordinary artists, the greatest of whom was Nat King Cole, who went from being a gifted jazz pianist who pioneered the trio format and occasionally sang to being one of the great baritones of post–World War II popular music. In 1953, the company scored its greatest coup by signing a supposed has-been, Frank Sinatra, whose last few albums with Columbia had flopped. Pairing him with arrangers Nelson Riddle, Billy May, and Gordon Jenkins once again made Sinatra the most influential popular singer in America.

In 1956, EMI's Sir Joseph Lockwood arranged with Wallichs, by then Capitol's principal owner, to buy 96 percent of the company. In 1961, one of the company's creative mainstays, Alan Livingston, became president, returning to the company after a five-year absence.

Livingston had a remarkable career. In 1946, he went to work at Capitol to develop its back catalog; later that year, he put out a kids' album called *Bozo at the Circus* that introduced the Bozo the Clown character (first portrayed

81

by Livingston himself), sold millions, and spawned a franchise. Later, he cowrote Mel Blanc's novelty hit "I Taut I Taw a Puddy Tat," based on the character voices Blanc created for Warner Brothers cartoons. Livingston and A&R chief Voyle Gilmore were the ones who signed Sinatra and convinced him to work with Nelson Riddle, with whom he made his most unforgettable albums, including *Frank Sinatra Sings for Only the Lonely.* As a TV executive from 1956 to 1961, Livingston's success wasn't as prolific, although he did produce the pilot for *Bonanza*, the biggest hit on American television during the early 1960s.

"When EMI bought Capitol, we made an agreement between us," Livingston told Beatles historian Bruce Spizer. "We had right of first refusal, and they the same in reverse, on any of EMI's English artists, or any artists around the world that they had. . . . Of course it worked very well for EMI because we had Nat Cole and we had many of the big bands who did very well. However, we were not successful with English records. Occasionally some hit would come out of France or even India but we just never got off the ground with English artists."

Dexter was in charge of reviewing all foreign material. He'd volunteered for the job as soon as the sale to EMI was made. (He may have been on shaky ground with domestic acts, since in his book, *Playback*—which is so pissy, its alternate title might be *Payback*—he recounts that the one time he pressed to be in the studio with Sinatra, "the intemperate and intransigent Hoboken baritone roared his refusal to work with me.") Dexter had some success, because in the 1950s, even after Elvis's arrival, American listeners were much more wide open to the music of the rest of the world. He issued Edith Piaf's version of Leiber and Stoller's "Black Denim Trousers and Motorcycle Boots" (which flopped, though Piaf had a top-10 single on Capitol with another song), and also got a top-10 single out of another French artist, Franck Pourcel.

He didn't try releasing many British records. He did so successfully only once, with Laurie London's "He's Got the Whole World in His Hands," a number-one single in 1958. He found an obscure album track, "Swingin' Sweethearts," by the even more obscure Ron Goodwin, and Capitol's promo staff brought it to number 52 on the charts. With England's biggest and best pre-Beatles British rock act, Cliff Richard and the Shadows, Capitol, thanks to Dexter, tried only twice, and both records flopped, albeit one of the US releases, "Move It," was probably the best record Richard ever made (though tame by US standards).

As soon as the Beatles began having hits in England, EMI, not to mention Brian Epstein, George Martin, and the band, expected the American company to at least *try* to spread their success. Dexter was unyielding. He rejected "Love Me Do" and "Please Please Me" because, he wrote, he did not like John Lennon's harmonica play-ing. (It was the novelty of the Lennon harmonica bursts that made George Martin try releasing a record by the Beatles.) The reasoning given in *Playback* for rejecting "She Loves You" is nonexistent. Dexter seems to have convinced himself that rock'n'roll really had been a flash in the pan, even though Capitol's best-selling act was a rock band, the Beach Boys. And he had long known that the wind had changed. In *Playback*, he describes a 1950 encounter with a 16-year-old girl from Hollywood High, who told him: "I only know Bullmoose Jackson is my kind of music. And I know I can't find my music on any of the regular labels. If it's on Decca or Columbia or Cap-itol, I don't want it. They only make music for old folks."

"The revolution had begun" is his only comment in the book. But every revolution contains within it the seeds of the counterrevolution, and Dexter was determinedly loyal to his concept that the greatest music in the world was jazz before bebop, and that "the most chronically tone-deaf slob on the block could be transformed into a raving jazz fanatic if he took just one evening of his life and, with the guidance of a selected stack of records and a patient instructor, assimilated the fine points of the art with an open mind and heart."

The facts showing otherwise did not deter him. Dexter was as committed to his version of reality as a Cuban exile who's lived for 40 years in Miami. He was more than will-ing to cut off Capitol's nose to spite rock'n'roll's face.

The real question is, How did Dave Dexter retain such control over the fate of the Beatles' American record releases? His tenure, from 1963 to 1966, covers by far the most important part of the Beatles' career. He not only delayed their appearance on a major label in this country for more than a year, he then proceeded to fiddle with every product that the Beatles sent to the States, not only making weird and inexcusable judgments about song choices and sequences but also doing a very bad job of getting the music he was sent mixed and mastered for final release. (Comparing American pressings to British pressings of the same songs is not a pretty experience for Yanks.)

How did he get away with it? The most elementary answer is that nobody in a position of authority over Dexter listened. Once EMI forced Dexter's boycott to end, nobody at Capitol who did listen had any background in rock that enabled them to make an astute judgment of what he was doing. (The domestic A&R staff rejected the Chiffons' "One Fine Day" in December 1962.) After that, nobody cared because they were too busy raking in the dough.

"One day I held the weekly A&R meeting, which I went to even though I was president, but I had come up through A&R so I had an interest in these meetings," Livingston told Spizer in *The Beatles Are Coming!* "I would decide, with the producers' help, which records to release, which artists to sign, what elements to put together and so forth. I had been reading the English music press, and I read about the success of a group called the Beatles. So I said to Dexter, 'What about the Beatles? Shouldn't we put them out?' He said, 'Alan, they're a bunch of long-haired kids. They're nothing. Forget it.' I thought that was OK. We hadn't had any success with English artists so why should I question him?

"Two weeks later I asked again because there was so much going on in England and he said, 'Alan, please, they're nothing. Forget it.' So we passed on them. We passed on the right of first refusal so EMI then went trying to find another place to get them to put their records out. They took the Beatles to CBS, then Columbia Records, to RCA, then RCA Victor records, to Decca Records, which in those days was a very big company, and every one of them turned them down.

"They finally found a small company in Philadelphia called Swan Records, who put out two sides. Two records and nothing happened, so Swan gave them up. They didn't want them any more. EMI then got Vee Jay Records, a very small company in serious financial trouble, black-owned. It was a free album to them, so they said, 'OK, we'll put it out.' And they couldn't pay the [royalties due] to EMI, so [they] lost their rights. They didn't seem to care because the album didn't sell; nothing happened. And that was the end of it. The Beatles could have been dead in the United States."

Livingston got it backward—the Vee-Jay releases came first—but other than that, what he says shows the complete absence of respect with which the Beatles were treated, and for that matter, the complete lack of respect for the British owners. The clearest thing about the attitude of Livingston and the rest of Capitol's A&R staff was that none of them except Dexter listened to the Beatles—not once, not ever—until Sir Joseph Lockwood demanded it.

If they had listened, no one in Capitol's executive offices would have known a damned thing about the rhythm and blues and soul music on which the Beatles based so much of their early sound, much less about the R&B/soul area of the record business. ("One Fine Day" became a number-one hit, and the group had several other big records.)

Vee-Jay Records, based in Chicago and owned by husband and wife Vivian Carter and James Bracken, was Motown before Motown, a black-owned company with an array of fine soul and R&B singers, including some with "crossover" appeal to white audiences, such as Jerry Butler, Betty Everett, and Gene Chandler. In addition, Vee-Jay had things Motown did not ever have. It made important records with such urban but not urbane bluesmen as Jimmy Reed and John Lee Hooker. It had perhaps the most important gospel catalog of the early 1960s. And it even had a hit act composed of white guys, the Four Seasons, whose "Sherry" and "Big Girls Don't Cry" falsetto doo-wop transported to another dimension with pop arrangements, broke into the American top-10 at just about the time that Dexter was finding the Beatles just a bunch of long-haired kids without commercial appeal.

Vee-Jay's promotion men were so skilled at getting records on the radio that it's not unlikely they might have broken through with the Beatles, as they had with the Four Seasons—if only EMI and the Beatles had lived up to their long-term contract.

EMI came to Vee-Jay as a last resort. Even the biggest R&B label, Atlantic, had turned them down, even though the company frequently put out records by white artists. (Co-owner Jerry Wexler reportedly argued that the music was not "pure.") EMI knew something about Vee-Jay: It distributed the label's records to the world outside the United States and the two companies used the same New York attorney, Paul Marshall. Marshall made the Beatles' deal with Vee-Jay without even telling Joseph Zerga, EMI's man nominally in charge on the East Coast. EMI also licensed to Vee-Jay another 1963 UK number one that Dexter decided Capitol couldn't use, Frank Ifield's "I Remember You," a remake of a Jimmy Dorsey song from 1942. The Vee-Jay release reached number five on the US charts.

So licensing the Beatles to Vee-Jay was not a complete crapshoot for EMI. The contract was a five-year agreement, with Vee-Jay to be given a six-month sell-off period if it were terminated early. If the deal had been maintained, it would have been Vee-Jay, owned by its creators, a black couple who originally ran a small record shop in Gary, Indiana, that made the initial profits from the biggest musical act in history rather than Capitol, owned by EMI, which called itself "the greatest recording company in the world."

Could the Beatles have been as profitable, prolific, and world changing on a label begun in Vivian and James Bracken's mom-and-pop record shop?

One's immediate thought is no—the difference in clout alone would have prevented it. But unlike Capitol, Vee-Jay at least understood the music well enough to release three of the first four singles that Capitol rejected. Also, Vee-Jay had shown that it could sell millions of records in the "white" pop marketplace; it had done so with the Four Seasons.

(It's delightful to think of the Rolling Stones, hard-core blues fans, and their impresario Andrew Loog Oldham being on the same label as John Lee Hooker and the Swan Silvertones. They'd have swooned at the possibility—as it was, they once recorded at Chess Records, directly across Chicago's Michigan Avenue from Vee-Jay's headquarters.)

Most important, Capitol had little or nothing to do with the Beatles' success in America. The company had planned to release "I Want to Hold Your Hand," to which it claimed to have renewed rights based on Vee-Jay's failure to send royalty statements for earlier records, in mid-January 1964. (Which means that the single probably still wasn't among the company's highest priorities, for Capitol had forgone the Thanksgiving-to-Christmas sales period, when up to 40 percent of all records were then sold.)

Brian Epstein made Livingston promise to spend

$50,000 promoting "I Want to Hold Your Hand," and Livingston told him he would, but no one thinks the company spent anywhere near that much, for the simple reason that the biggest expense in promoting a single is to get it on the radio. "I Want to Hold Your Hand" got played on the radio so quickly that Capitol/EMI tried to get it taken off!

At the urging of a fan, Marsha Albert, disc jockey Carroll James of WWDC in Washington, DC, obtained a copy of the UK pressing (brought to him by an airline stewardess) and began playing it on December 17, almost a month before the original release date. (He brought Albert into the studio and let her introduce it the first time, but after that, it was his "exclusive.") James also sent copies to colleagues around the country, and the record began to take off in Chicago and St. Louis as well.

EMI tried to stop this airplay. When EMI's American attorney called James and then sent him a telegram ordering him to cease and desist airplay, the disc jockey told the lawyer, "Look, you can't stop me from playing it. The record is a hit. It's a major thing." EMI surrendered and began making plans to get many more records than it had initially anticipated into the stores in January.

Vee-Jay certainly could have done *that*. It, too, could have had key promo men humiliate themselves by wearing Beatles wigs as they went from station to station. And while the prime peril for an independent record company, one without deep capital reserves or backing, is to have a hit without a follow-up, there were four follow-ups already sitting in the Vee-Jay catalog.

Chances are that the Beatles would have had a more empathetic relationship with their record label if it had been Vee-Jay, since that company and its chief producer, Calvin Carter (Vivian Bracken's brother), made exactly the kind of American pop–R&B records that the group most admired.

But Vee-Jay didn't get that chance, and so instead of working with a team that also promoted Hooker and the Seasons and Butler and the Five Blind Boys of Mississippi, they wound up working with a company that promoted the Beach Boys, Nat King Cole, orchestras that Jackie Gleason pretended to conduct, and the Kingston Trio.

———

Mainly, the blame for Vee-Jay losing the Beatles belongs to Vee-Jay itself.

The company had three problems. First, its president, Ewart Abner, the company's business manager since 1955 and its president since 1961, had never created a genuine business accounting system. As his successor, Randy Wood, told R&B historian Arnold Shaw, "Ewart Abner had the whole thing in his head. And how you can run a company that's doing $2 to $3 million a year—keeping the facts and figures in your head—is an enigma. I guess he had that sixth sense of knowing what to put where, which is, perhaps, [one of] the qualities that make a president. But they also serve to fuck up that company pretty badly. And to add to everything else, we had Internal Revenue threatening to close us up on an almost daily basis. We had four or five creditors threatening to throw us into bankruptcy. And our comptroller said, 'Go ahead, we'll beat you to the courtyard and do it ourselves.'"

Second, one probable reason for not keeping sound, transparent books (or paying taxes) was that the company had been drained of $300,000 to $400,000. Abner originally claimed the missing money had gone for payola to disc jockeys, but it developed that he had significant gambling debts in Las Vegas and had "borrowed" the company's money to pay them off. The Brackens decided to keep this quiet, although Abner left the company. (He'd return as president in 1965, a pretty light penance for such malfeasance.)

By spring 1963, Vee-Jay's cash-flow crisis was so great that the company fell behind on payroll taxes and the federal excise tax (applicable to vinyl records because they were manufactured petroleum products) and got into a royalty dispute with the Four Seasons. Among the projected projects the label canceled was an album called *Introducing the Beatles.*

Nor did Vee-Jay pay royalties to EMI for Frank Ifield ($6,571) or the Beatles (a meager $859), or even issue royalty statements. On August 8, 1963, a telegram from Paul Marshall to Vee-Jay read: "Require you immediately cease manufacture and distribution of any and all records containing performances of Frank Ifield or the Beatles STOP Please confirm that all manufacture has stopped and all masters and pressings recalled and destroyed." EMI regarded this as a valid unilateral termination of their contract with Vee-Jay.

Bruce Spizer believes that EMI took this step because it feared Vee-Jay might go out of business, rendering the rights to the Beatles and Ifield recordings inaccessible. But Brian Epstein and the Beatles desperately wanted US success, and EMI also wanted Capitol to get its head out of its ass on the matter. Termination of Vee-Jay's rights returned to Capitol the right of first refusal. On December 4, 1963, Capitol issued a press release trumpeting its acquisition of the Beatles and plans to release a blockbuster single, "I Want to Hold Your Hand" backed with "I Saw Her Standing There."

Vee-Jay began to realize what was at stake after that, and particularly after an article about Capitol's plans for the group appeared in *Billboard*, the music industry's leading trade paper. Discussion at the crisis board meetings began to revolve around the Beatles. Someone remembered that the company had not only the singles and album masters, but also 6,000 cover slicks for the *Introducing the Beatles* album aborted the previous summer.

A major problem was that nobody at Vee-Jay, including attorney Walter Hofer, had a copy of the contract with EMI's American agent, Transglobal. They were utterly in the dark as to what they could and could not do legally. (Why didn't they tell their attorney for the deal, Paul Marshall, to get them a copy of the papers? Possibly because exposing Marshall's conflict of interest might itself void the contract, which was in EMI's favor, not theirs.)

But that's the record business, a fly-by-night affair in many respects now, let alone in the early 1960s. The Vee-Jay executives decided they had no choice but to push ahead and release *Introducing* in the first week of the New Year. "We have to take a chance on the Beatles," Jay Lasker, recently appointed president, said to the assembled executives. What he meant was that the cash crisis causing so much trouble in December would by February capsize the label altogether.

EMI and Transglobal certainly had copies of the licensing agreement. As written, if Vee-Jay had complied with all terms, the company would have had the right to continue issuing the singles it had put out but not the album, even though the masters had been delivered, since it had not used a "timely right of first refusal" to issue the British debut album.

Vee-Jay's Beatles album banged head-on into Capitol's. Vee-Jay also continued to promote and sell its Beatles singles. That was a big part of the reason that the Fab Four wound up with singles in all five top slots on the *Billboard* chart shortly thereafter. It was also a very visible signal that the situation was a legal thicket.

Capitol next went to Chicago's Cook County circuit

court to ask for a temporary restraining order, and eventual permanent injunction, against Vee-Jay making, distributing, or selling any further Beatles product. Its argument was principally that Vee-Jay had failed to issue royalty statements and pay amounts due on the singles it had released and then further botched the agreement between the two labels by failing to issue *Introducing the Beatles* for almost a year after receiving the master tapes in March 1963. It also argued, as record companies always do in cases involving rights to artists, that commercial success in the music world is fleeting, a matter of weeks or months, which made it imperative to assure that its control of the music was exclusive while the window of opportunity remained open.

Capitol wanted all the tapes back; Vee-Jay responded that it couldn't find the tapes due to the change in management, but that when it found them, it would turn them over.

Unbelievably, Vee-Jay's Chicago attorney failed to make any affirmative argument. He didn't even file a written answer. Nor did he argue for discovery of documents—such as the contract between Vee-Jay and Transglobal!—and he didn't ask the court to take into consideration the slow payment practices common in the record business. He didn't even mention that EMI's Transglobal was itself in arrears in issuing statements and checks for its international distribution of Vee-Jay records! (Vee-Jay was undoubtedly owed a hell of a lot more than $859, since its international records were often successes while every American Beatles release had flopped.)

He did argue that Vee-Jay shouldn't be sued by EMI or Capitol because its deal was with Transglobal; that the deal was valid and therefore it was Capitol, not Vee-Jay, that had no Beatles rights; and that Capitol had full knowledge of Vee-Jay's contract with Transglobal and thus didn't have "clean hands." (In the *record* business?) He also attempted to introduce a new complaint, filed in New York State against Capitol (and Swan, since under the terms of the contract with Transglobal, "She Loves You" should also have come out on Vee-Jay). He wanted this complaint to replace an answer to the immediate allegations. No way, said the judge.

Judge Cornelius J. Harrington decided in Capitol's favor—he had no choice. Without any counterargument to work with, the legal effect was that the Capitol arguments were "uncontested" and therefore to be dealt with as true. Besides that, there was an answering document filed by Vee-Jay's codefendant, Transglobal. As a subsidiary of EMI, of which Capitol was also an offspring, Transglobal "admitted" everything that Capitol had alleged. So Judge Harrington issued a temporary restraining order, also called an injunction, against Vee-Jay's manufacture or distribution of Beatles records.

Bruce Spizer, who practiced law before becoming a Beatles scholar and author, believes that had Vee-Jay's attorney presented any kind of acceptable answering document at all, the situation would have been reversed: "If Vee-Jay had filed an answer denying Capitol's allegations that the licensing agreement terminated on August 8, 1963, the Chicago court would have denied Capitol's motion because the licensing agreement would have been at issue. Vee-Jay would have been allowed to continue selling Beatles records during the pendency of a trial on the merits, which would have taken months to resolve."

So, in the spring of 1964, when the *Second Album* was released, the Beatles had records out on three different labels and three lawsuits, thanks to a suit filed against Vee-Jay by Capitol-owned publishing company Beechwood Music over the music publishing rights to "Love Me Do" and "P.S. I Love You," which were on *Introducing*. Vee-Jay would have lost the Beechwood case under any circumstances. US copyright law gives the author the right to determine first issue of a song in America, and those two tracks had not been properly licensed. (Vee-Jay didn't even ask for permission until January 9, 1964.)

Vee-Jay retained New York attorney Walter Hofer, an experienced music business practitioner, and things got more interesting. Hofer made an intriguing argument. He said that the Beatles were *not* a flash in the pan: "They have been popular for quite a few years in England, not in the United States; not as popular in the United States. And it is not something that will be here today and gone tomorrow." He may have been the first person in America to figure this out, or at least to say so in public.

Injunction ping-pong went on for the next several months, with the temporary restraining order first being lifted, then reinstated, then lifted again and reinstated again, several times over. Meanwhile the Vee-Jay executives scrambled to keep the company's insolvency from capsizing it entirely. By continuing to fight the lawsuit, Vee-Jay got the injunction lifted often enough to continue making and selling Beatles records for the next few months, a life-or-death difference.

After an appellate court lifted the restraining order in early February, Vee-Jay still couldn't get around the Beechwood mess. So it did the logical thing: released a version of *Introducing the Beatles* that did not contain "P.S. I Love You" and "Love Me Do." It also released a single of "Twist and Shout" on its subsidiary label, Tollie.

Introducing the Beatles sold very well, as it should have, since consumers cared only about music, not rights. The only song that *Meet the Beatles*, the first American Capitol album, and *Introducing the Beatles* have in common is "I Saw Her Standing There." *Introducing* also featured the Beatles' immediately famous "Twist and Shout," which didn't appear on a Capitol album for more than a year. The ready availability of 11 additional Beatles tracks that Capitol couldn't provide made *Introducing* a major hit—Vee-Jay had planned an initial pressing of 30,000, but wound up shipping 80,000 copies that first week. "Don't wait," Vee-Jay president Randy Wood telegraphed his distributors. "This is best seller since Presley days." Eventually, *Introducing the Beatles* sold about 1.4 million copies, a huge bestseller.

It's hard to figure how aggrieved the Beatles felt about this shambles. In any event, at their Hollywood Bowl concert on August 23, 1964, the band met backstage with Randy Wood and accepted a kind of gold record for *Introducing the Beatles*—not a "real" gold album, because Vee-Jay didn't belong to the industry trade group that issues official ones, the now-notorious Recording Industry Association of America. One wonders whether the Beatles were struck by a black man's being the president of their previous record label, an uncommon situation (to say the least) in 1964.

Selling a million Beatles albums and a huge number of singles couldn't drag Vee-Jay out of its downward arc. Before 1964 ended, there was no trial of either case. Instead, a settlement of all the cases occurred, its terms very much in Capitol's favor. By June 1965, the Brackens had fired Wood and appointed as Vee-Jay's new chief executive Ewart Abner.

In August 1966, a federal court refused to allow

Vee-Jay to enter voluntary bankruptcy and took control of its remaining assets. But, according to Wood, the bankruptcy managers appointed by the court gave up on trying to sort out what rights it legally held. "Almost thirteen years of the company could not be pieced together, except by two people, Abner or myself," he told Shaw. "The courts tried for a solid year to sell, but they couldn't dispose of the company free and clear; they could sell only on the basis of right, title, and interest. The court could not warrant that Vee Jay owned many things—they weren't sure."

Wood and a partner finally bought the assets. Those records eventually became the property of Motown Records and are now owned by Universal, the conglomerate that bought Motown from the perpetually solvent Berry Gordy, cowriter of Barrett Strong's "Money."

Even in April 1964, when *The Beatles' Second Album* hit the stores and the charts and millions of teenage brains, Capitol Records had clearly become the band's sole American record company. The best chance Vee-Jay ever had—given that it was fighting not only Capitol but its own international distributor, EMI—was a settlement that paid off well enough to keep it in business. But the only way it could accomplish that was by cutting off Capitol's supply of Beatles sales, and with the Beatles churning out great music at the pace of a revolution, that couldn't happen.

I still think it's plausible that Vee-Jay would have done a better creative job with the Beatles and a serviceable one in marketing and promoting them (given that the group effectively did all its own promotion and marketing by continuing to exist and make records). But that is a thought experiment, not a practical assessment.

Military historian Carl von Clausewitz argued that in war, defense is the stronger force with the weaker object, while attack is the weaker force but a stronger object. This presumes a war between forces that are roughly equal, however. The problem with the cat-and-mouse game that Vee-Jay played was that the cat was the largest recording organization in the world and Vee-Jay was not even a very big mouse.

You could also make the case that facing hostility and stupidity from its American record company (which was allowed by its English record company) gave the Beatles more incentive to break with standard record business (and record-making) processes.

What turned out to be most relevant was not so much that Capitol won control over the golden goose the company had tried to starve to death, but that the Beatles got nothing out of the situation. Capitol came through not only as the Beatles' exclusive record company in the world's largest record market, but also in control of the contents of the group's American records. Capitol's priorities, not those of the Beatles, shaped all American Beatles albums until 1967, when *Sgt. Pepper's Lonely Hearts Club Band* presented a project that not even greed and loathing could alter (as the band's new contract ensured).

The Beatles lived with the consequences, prosperously but not altogether happily.

6

BUTCHERED

Record companies exist for a single reason: to make money. Music is simply their vehicle for making money. Remember this fact, and much that seems opaque comes clear; forget it, and you're lost in a fog that's less like a reverie than a delusion. The motive, somewhere at the beginning or end of the chain, often both, is an extra buck of profit. (We will not speak of the artists, whether his lust for the gold lamé suit or hers for the pink Cadillac—at least not yet.) Without profit, the record company withers and dies, like a starved human being.

You may say that this isn't an observation about the record industry, it's an observation about all corporations. I might add that it is not even my observation, its origin lies with Adam Smith and Karl Marx. But with "artistic" endeavors, this elementary concept is often forgotten. Remember it, and you can see that in the most fundamental respect, Capitol Records was not different from Vee-Jay Records or, for that matter, from the Beatles' own Apple.

So to understand the most basic aspects of why Capitol Records did what it did to the Beatles albums it released prior to *Sgt. Pepper's Lonely Hearts Club Band* you need to understand the profit issues involved. There are good guys and bad guys in the tale. The profit motive can't explain everything. But if you jump to the conclusion that a good nature or a bad one is why people did what they did, you'll end up with foolish answers to pretty simple questions.

To start with: Why did Capitol Records reject the first four Beatles singles? Why did they reject the fifth one and then release it after all?

Because the person making the decision was an idiot is a correct answer, but not a particularly useful one.

Here's a better way to spin it:

The person appointed to decide which of EMI's non-US records should be released by its US subsidiary, Capitol, persuaded himself that releasing Beatles singles in America would never be profitable. But that was belief, not proof. "I Want to Hold Your Hand" came out on Capitol because EMI needed to know definitively if the Beatles could profit the company in the United States at the level they did in the United Kingdom. So EMI insisted that the record be released even if the opinion of Capitol's international director of A&R or even Capitol's chief executive was that promoting the Beatles in America was a guaranteed economic bust.

The idiot in question was Dave Dexter Jr. He wasn't an idiot because he didn't like rock'n'roll. He was an idiot because he used his hatred of rock'n'roll to convince himself that the Beatles had no commercial potential. (He seems to have deluded himself into believing that if only he and other gatekeepers would keep to sufficiently high standards, the big bands and his glory days would return in a golden cart from the cloudless heavens.)

In this case, Dexter wasn't any bigger an idiot than Atlantic's Jerry Wexler, one of the greatest record producers and evaluators who ever lived. Wexler also couldn't hear any commercial potential in the Beatles, which is pretty idiotic, and even more so if Wexler's explanation was that the Beatles weren't "pure" (pure what?)—unless he just said that to get whoever from EMI sent to peddle them off the phone.

Nevertheless, it wasn't anyone's disdain for the Beatles that led to the alternate universes that are the Beatles' British and American album catalogs. If Dave Dexter had never existed, and if Capitol had regarded those initial Beatles albums and their track sequences and running lengths as the Grail, it *still* wouldn't have released the same albums in both countries.

I state this with such certainty because doing that would have cost Capitol a bundle.

The economics of British record companies are significantly different from those of American ones.

In Britain, record companies pay songwriters and music publishers (but not performers) for each album from a fixed pool of money, the sum depending on the number of records sold. That pool is then divided by the number of songs on the album: If an album has 14 tracks, each song is worth $\frac{1}{14}$th of the pool. If the album contains 11 songs, each publisher gets $\frac{1}{11}$th. It doesn't profit the record company at all to reduce the number of songs on an album.

In the United States, by law, the maximum amount each writer and publisher receives is fixed. From 1913 to 1972, the amount was set at 2¢ per track. (Lower rates could be negotiated.) If an album had 14 tracks, the record label paid out 28¢ per album sold; if there were 12 tracks, they paid 24¢; if 11 tracks, 22¢. This gave record companies great incentive to reduce the number of songs on an album.

Not only that, reducing the number of songs saved a US record company money in a way that went directly to profit. It cost a negligible amount extra, then as now, to prepare 14 tracks for an album rather than 12. It cost absolutely nothing more to manufacture or package more tracks. By releasing albums with only 12 tracks, the typical number, Capitol retained an additional 4¢ per unit compared to a 14-song album. By releasing all early

Beatles albums except *Meet the Beatles* with only *11* tracks, Capitol gained a total of 6¢.

American record companies could also save money on artist royalties by releasing albums with fewer tracks, since many contracts calculated the artist's share of income per song performed.

That's how the Beatles were paid, and at a pathetic rate, too. In 1962, George Martin signed them to EMI's Parlophone label, which he ran, for a royalty of one English penny per side (a side is one track, in this case). They also received an escalation of one farthing per year. A farthing was one-quarter of a penny, or roughly $1/1,000$th of a pound. (There had once been a farthing coin, but its value diminished so much that it was taken out of circulation in 1956.) A British pound sterling then contained 240 pennies. In 1964, one pound had a fixed value of $2.80. At that rate, a 14-song album cost Capitol (in rounded numbers) 24.5¢ in artist royalties; an 11-track album cost it 19.25¢.

Taken together with song publishing royalties of two cents per track, that means Capitol "earned" 11.25¢ more per album sold by selling its own concoctions rather than the lengthier British originals. The difference is $117,500 profit per million albums sold.

Meet the Beatles did have the standard American 12 songs, so Capitol earned only 7.75¢ extra by not releasing the 14-track Beatles debut album, *Please Please Me*, or $77,500 per million. *Meet the Beatles* sold about five million copies, an extra profit of $387,500. *The Beatles' Second Album* sold about two million copies, netting Capitol an extra $235,000, again pure profit. (Remember also that 1964 dollars had more than twice the spending power of the early 21st-century dollar.) The label made such profit on every Beatles album it released until *Sgt. Pepper's.*

That's only one of the ways that shorter albums increased Capitol's profits. It also used the extra tracks from the British albums along with singles and material from British EPs ("extended play" singles containing three to five songs) to make up new albums.

British singles generally didn't appear on albums, but the practice isn't universal: *Please Please Me* has both sides of what were then the Beatles' only two singles. In any event, singles were not part of other UK Beatles albums.

In America, the idea of leaving singles off an album was inconceivable. The more hits a group had on an album, it was felt, the more copies were likely to be sold. This alone would have driven Capitol to release Beatles albums in a different version.

There was also virtually no market in the United States for EPs, although Capitol did try releasing a couple of the Beatles' during the peak of Beatlemania, one in 1964 (which charted at number 92) and one in 1965 (which charted at 68). That didn't mean the EP material wasn't valuable. It was immensely valuable because it could be incorporated into the additional albums Capitol pieced together.

Capitol's strategy was to take the three songs per British album it failed to release and combine them with various EP and single tracks that were not on any British album to create entirely new LPs having the delightful added advantage of even more extra profits, since there were only 11 tracks on the albums it made up, too. Between Capitol's first bowdlerization, *Meet the Beatles* in 1964, and *Revolver* in 1966, which was the last bowdlerized album, Parlophone released seven Beatles albums in England. In America over the same time, Capitol released 10 Beatles albums. It would be hard to calculate the additional profit these three albums generated, but we can get a general idea from the example above using the *Second Album* and *Meet the Beatles*.

Only the fact that the conceptual integrity of the material on *Sgt. Pepper's Lonely Hearts Club Band* was its main selling point (and Brian Epstein's finally negotiating a better recording contract for the band) stopped Capitol from continuing the practice of putting together hodgepodge LPs.

Not that the Beatles didn't try to end it sooner. All the Beatles complained about the way the American record company dealt with the band's album catalog. "When the American company released albums like *Yesterday . . .*

and Today, we didn't have anything to do with them," said George. "They always put out more albums in the States. If we put out two singles and two albums, they'd convert them to three albums by keeping the extra tracks."

Especially from about *Help!* onward, the band's hostility became more evident. By the time four tracks were excised from *Rubber Soul* and two unrelated ones added, and *Revolver* was remodeled by removing four of its original songs and adding two unrelated ones, it was clear that the Beatles were being fucked with: No one in control at Capitol paid even lip service to their creation of concept albums. It was inexcusable to make those cuts.

The Beatles always denied that the famous "butcher cover" for the 1966 odds-and-ends album, *Yesterday . . . and Today*, commented upon Capitol's hacking up their albums for profit (and doing it with an unmistakable ignorance of and/or contempt for whatever artistry the Beatles might be displaying in the album medium).

The official version is that the famous "butcher cover"—a photo of the Beatles dressed as butchers, surrounded by raw meat and dismembered baby dolls—for *Yesterday . . . and Today* didn't have a thing to do with sending a message to Capitol about their hatred of the company's practice of chopping up their records.

It's even true that they hired Robert Whitaker, one of Lennon's art school chums, to photograph them precisely because when they'd last posed for photos—in the session that produced the cover of the American album *Beatles*

'65—they'd looked listless and exhausted. ("They stuck an awful-looking photo of us looking just deadbeat but supposed to be a happy-go-lucky foursome," says Lennon in the DVD *Anthology*.) They came across with nothing like the energy that had animated them into the Top of the Pops.

Whitaker has developed a remarkable spiel about the meaning of the photo sequence, which he titled "A Somnambulant Adventure" (". . . The sausages are meant to be an umbilical cord. And then that image was going to be inset inside a pregnant woman's womb . . ."), that would sound like bullshit in its entirety if you didn't know anything about the pretensions of the Beatles and the people surrounding them after LSD came into their lives. (The whole of "A Somnambulant Adventure" can be seen in Whitaker's book, *The Unseen Beatles*. He never worked for the Beatles again.)

But when asked about the butcher photographs at the time, the band never mentioned "A Somnambulant Adventure." Instead, they talked about Vietnam.

"It's as relevant as Vietnam," said Lennon during the band's last concert tour in the summer of 1966. "If the public can accept something as cruel as the war, they can accept this cover."

"It's their comment on war," said Brian Epstein, who hated the butcher pictures so much that he told Alan Livingston he'd like to burn every one of Whitaker's negatives. "That's what it means to them."

Livingston remembers Paul arguing in favor of the cover after the American company told the group that there had been near-universal rejection of the cover by both radio and retailers. "He was adamant and felt very strongly that we should go forward. He said, 'It's our comment on war.'" But what Livingston added next probably tolled the bell: "I don't know why it was a comment on war or if it would be interpreted that way."

One prominent American, *San Francisco Chronicle* jazz critic Ralph J. Gleason, saw exactly that: "Far from being offensive, the 'butcher boys' cover strikes me as a subtle protest against war, as well as an example of 'black humor.' Isn't there something paradoxical about the shrill reaction of disc jockeys and program directors to this cover at a time when the heads are being blown off real children and their bodies seared by American napalm in Vietnam?"

Gleason's column is particularly revealing because he cast the entire scandal as a battle between the Beatles and Capitol for control of their art. He believed that "Capitol's relationship with The Beatles, who re-signed for a reported $5 million less than a year ago, has been shaky for some time. 'This can cost Capitol the Beatles,' one knowledgeable record industry spokesman said this weekend."

(The only other favorable contemporary evaluation of the pictures came from George Osaki, Capitol's art director, who found the cover amusing as "a departure from the usual four smiling heads" and not offensive, since "the

Beatles weren't chopping things up." Even so, Beatles aide Tony Barrow claims that Osaki or his staff airbrushed out the red bloodstains on the white butcher's smocks they wore in the picture—so the butcher cover itself was a censored image!)

But the Beatles didn't have that much power—not yet, anyway. Capitol had sent 60,000 advance albums with the butcher image to radio stations, the press, and their sales staff at the branches Capitol maintained all over the country. The retailers refused to handle them. The disc jockeys started blasting the cover on the air, the first blow to the Beatles' universally cheery image (soon to be besmirched more vigorously by the "bigger than Jesus" tempest). Gleason said response was divided between uptight straights, who hated the cover, and "stoners," who got the joke. But the further you moved from San Francisco (or New York and a couple of other cities), the smaller the percentage of stoners.

Anyway, the butcher cover never really had a chance. "It was a matter of economics," as Livingston succinctly put it.

Capitol faced a second economic problem: It had already pressed and jacketed 1.2 million copies of *Yesterday . . . and Today*. Every one of the LPs had to be placed in a new jacket or the new cover pasted over the old photo. The new covers cost 15¢ each, and Capitol had to pay overtime wages to its entire workforce, from coast to coast, to come in over a weekend and fix each copy. The cost was reported to be about $250,000—not much considering the extra profit the company earned from each of the albums that the butcher cover protested, whether the Beatles intended it to or not.

Nobody—not the Beatles, Capitol, or for that matter the censorious record sellers and disc jockeys—came out of it looking good. The next summer, when *Sgt. Pepper's* was being readied for release, with its fantastic Peter Blake photomontage on the cover, Brian Epstein suggested the album be issued in a brown paper bag.

So, for Capitol, the idea of simply putting on American shelves the unadulterated British albums made no sense whatever.

Despite the attitude of today's Beatles fans, I don't think it ruined the chance of "properly understanding" the Beatles, either. *Please Please Me* and *With the Beatles* are not concept albums, except insofar as the latter tries to emulate the former in balancing John with Paul, originals with rock'n'roll classics, and nods to the front-man skills of George and Ringo. Both are based upon the repertoire and, to my ear anyway, some sense of the flow of the band's stage show. They are not particularly advanced examples of the state of record making in 1963. (They are, of course, advanced examples of the art of music making then.)

A portion of the significance of Lennon's throat bleeding as he sang "Twist and Shout" is lost in our awe at what he was willing to risk to express himself. Lennon wasn't bleeding because he pushed himself so hard. He was bleeding only because producer Martin had given over just one 12-hour day to make an album to exploit the first Beatles hit. Partly, that situation was forced upon Martin and the band by the group's heavy touring schedule, which was necessary to make a living. Lennon also had a cold, but there was nothing to be done about it—there was one day to do the work, February 11, 1963, and that was it.

The Beatles were not present when George Martin recorded the *Please Please Me* piano overdubs on March 20; they were not present when Martin did the mixing and mastering on March 25. It is unlikely that the Beatles were consulted on the track sequencing, or on the quality of Martin's mixes and mastering. They may have been consulted on the cover art, since Epstein's office supplied it. It is less likely that they were asked to approve the title.

The group began recording the album that became *With the Beatles* on July 18, 1963, and finished on October 23. In those three months, they spent all or part of seven working days in the studio, including one day (October 3) when all they attempted was Ringo's maracas overdub on "I Wanna Be Your Man" and three takes of "Little Child." They were not present for mixing or mastering. It is not known whether they had a hand in sequencing, which again seems to take its cue from their stage show, or in choosing the album title. The awesome cover photograph unquestionably came from the band's headquarters and, according to George, the idea was theirs and Robert Freeman based his work on photographs taken of the Beatles by Astrid Kirchherr in Hamburg.

Therefore, it is not reasonable to say that, by dismantling, reassembling, and rearranging this material, spreading it across *Meet the Beatles* and *The Beatles' Second Album*, Capitol Records and its international A&R man, Dave Dexter Jr., despoiled the Beatles' artistic intention. That thought is purely anachronistic, because it assumes that the kind of intentions the Beatles possessed on *Rubber Soul*, *Revolver*, and *Sgt. Pepper's Lonely Hearts Club Band* were already developed. They certainly were not. If anyone's intentions were violated in those cases, they were George Martin's, who was not quite a Beatle, no matter his piano licks on "Money."

It's hard to see how Capitol had a realistic choice in the matter. The American market did want the singles on the album—that meant the first one had to include "I Want to Hold Your Hand." Given how little information each LP could hold (about 35 minutes for the best sound reproduction), that meant that something else from the British album had to be left off. The American royalty system would not allow 14 tracks on the album, and that meant two more (in reality, three) had to go.

It's worth comparing *Please Please Me*, *Meet the Beatles*, and Vee-Jay's *Introducing the Beatles*. The only song from *Please Please Me* that's also on *Meet the Beatles* is "I Saw Her Standing There." *Introducing the Beatles*, in its first version, contained all but two songs ("Please Please Me" and "Ask Me Why") from the first British album, the other two presumably having been dropped because of the song-royalty situation. Yet no one argues that the first

Introducing the Beatles, which is to all intents and purposes the American version of *Please Please Me*, is vastly superior to *Meet the Beatles*. Which makes sense since it is not (you could make a good argument that it's better, but not by more than a hair—a hair split by Capitol's failure to include any of the Beatles' versions of rock'n'roll and R&B classics on *Meet the Beatles*).

The Early Beatles, a 1965 roundup of the early Beatles material that had been tied up in the Vee-Jay litigation, contains 11 tracks, all from *Please Please Me*. I've never heard that record championed as being vastly superior to *Meet the Beatles*, either. It shouldn't be, since based on its track listing, the album was sequenced by throwing the tape boxes in the air and starting with what landed on top. But *The Early Beatles* is more like *Please Please Me* than *Meet the Beatles* is.

Each of the Beatles' early albums has great music to offer and had something greater to give in 1964: the chance to discover the Beatles and their music, and all that went with those two things.

With the Beatles, the second UK album, was the source of 9 of the 12 tracks on *Meet the Beatles*—possibly because of the Vee-Jay *Introducing the Beatles* quagmire. So the die was cast: The Beatles' second American album (second on Capitol, at least) couldn't conform to the Beatles' second British album, because the first American album pretty much was the second British album. After that, there was probably a chance that one catchall album for leftovers and such could have been issued and then

Capitol would have been on the path of releasing the same albums as Parlophone.

But to accomplish that, Brian Epstein would have had to deal forcefully with the record companies. He would perhaps have had to tell George Martin to tell Sir Joseph Lockwood that the Beatles were not going to make any further recordings unless and until Capitol agreed to echo the group and Martin's releases. (Capitol would have still made huge profits since the Beatles outsold any other act on that label or any other by a million or more units per release.)

Brian Epstein wasn't that good a businessman (he didn't begin to renegotiate the band's stingy deal with EMI until 1965). He certainly wouldn't have wanted to slow down Beatlemania, which crested and crested and crested for the next two or three years (although he wouldn't really have had to slow it down, since EMI surely feared such an eventuality much more than the band did, and the request wasn't unreasonable anyway).

Epstein also might not have wanted to do that because it would have cost him and the band money. In the end, the Beatles made more by selling 10 albums with 11 tracks each in the United States than they would have by selling nine albums of 14 tracks each. It is not to cast shame on the Beatles that I point out that they were very eager to become rich and famous and, once rich and famous, to become richer, if not more famous. That strikes me as part and parcel of the ambition that let them achieve so much on the artistic plane.

There's a reason that even I wish the Beatles had convinced Epstein to make that call to Sir Joseph Lockwood, though. It has nothing to do with track orders, album titles, or intention. It has to do with the inferior sound quality of Capitol's American releases.

Audiophile Beatles fans refer to the sound of the Capitol albums as "Dexterized" because of the ludicrous amount of echo and other bogus "stereo" effects Dave Dexter used. The main result of Dexterization is loss of sonic balance, important details, warmth, and presence. The American mono masters are considerably better than the stereo (or "stereo") ones, but still not comparable to the British ones. The British Beatles masters were top-notch for their time, comparable to the quality achieved by, for instance, Holland–Dozier–Holland at Motown, Phil Spector at Philles, and the Beach Boys, who were also on Capitol, and were also subject to bogus stereo mixes, although at least theirs were labeled "Duophonic," not "Stereophonic."

Why Dexter messed with the material he received from England isn't apparent. He doesn't discuss the issue in his book *Playback*, except to say how much the Beatles told him they liked his alterations. It's probable that his monkeyshines were the combined product of his disdain for the music and his extreme self-importance (which glares off virtually every page in *Playback*). To understand that, you need to know more about Dave Dexter.

7

THE MAN WHO HATED THE BEATLES

The whole idea that Dave Dexter Jr. became a figure of any consequence in the Beatles story reeks of myth and fable. That circumstances forced it, that he didn't do anything his bosses didn't want done, hardly matters. Dexter managed to mark everything he did with (some would say "to") the Beatles with a deep personal signature.

I don't mean he operated with élan or panache. I mean Dexter left a deep personal signature like a schoolboy with a jackknife on a desktop. What he did wasn't always atrocious, but it was rarely less than inappropriate. The *Second Album* stands as Dexter's monument, the finest pastiche he created from what was the Beatles' catalog in their native land.

But to tell Dave Dexter Jr.'s story completely also requires an indictment.

And not only an indictment of Dave Dexter Jr. What

could the clowns who ran Capitol Records have been *thinking*? Here's a guy whose single-handed decision cost them the first four Beatles singles—and we have only his word to go on that he wouldn't have rejected the fifth. Does he get demoted? No. Does he get fired? Nope.

He gets given the assignment of putting together albums made from the materials at hand. Other than making sure that all available recent hit singles appeared as soon as possible on these LPs, he seems to have had few or no guidelines. Nobody claims he had any supervision. On three albums, Dexter actually gives himself a production credit: "Produced in England by George Martin and in the U.S.A. with the assistance of Dave Dexter, Jr.," read the sleeves of *Something New* and *Beatles '65*. "Produced in England by George Martin and in the U.S.A. by Dave Dexter, Jr.," it says on *Help!* Maybe there Dexter deserved a notice that he was responsible. He had taken tapes of the background score material and intercut them with several of the songs from the movie to create that album. Further, he did this in one night, all the while bitching bitterly, and then was chewed out by the boss, Alan Livingston, for the quality of the thing, which has as much relation to the UK *Help!* as horsemeat does to Kobe beef. But Capitol eagerly—greedily—slapped it into the marketplace.

No reason to envy Dexter the task of reassembling the Beatles' output. The band was bound to resent it. No one would have anticipated when he was putting together the *Second Album* or maybe even *Help!* that large numbers of

American fans would one day be able to make direct comparisons with the British releases. It wasn't exactly Dexter's fault that he had to chop four tracks from the English *Rubber Soul* and three from the UK *Revolver*, albums with beautifully conceived internal integrity. True, someone with a slight sensitivity to what the band was trying to accomplish might have gone to his bosses and said, "I know what the economics are, but this is the Beatles and these are concept albums. Let's forgo a little dough." But that wasn't Dexter. It wasn't jazz so it was shit, and since he was no longer permitted to flush it, he got it out of the house as quick as could be.

You could even say that Dexter didn't quite butcher *Rubber Soul*—he turned it into a voguish folk-rock album, which sounds fine to me, but this time the Beatles had had an intent, and folk rock wasn't it—or anyway, not all of it.

Even if you like the song selection on some of the records—*Second Album*, *Rubber Soul*, *Beatles '65* all work for me—Dexter's approach couldn't be condoned. He altered the sound of every album he revamped, probably by remastering, although he may have also had access to tapes that would allow remixing to be done. (It is *extremely* unlikely that he overdubbed any parts, though. Where instruments inaudible on the British masters are heard on the American records, it's almost always because Capitol was sent a different master take or mix.)

In any event, the soundscape changed. Dexter made the records "wetter," in particular adding a heavy dose of reverb (a type of echo) and equalization (a way of proportioning high and low frequencies) to them. Like too much salt, the result can give you a headache. If you have something better to compare it with, it can also curdle your stomach. As producer Eric Ambel comments, "Adding reverb to any finished mix is editorializing the music. Adding reverb is not a usual part of 'remastering.'" To almost everyone, the British Beatles records sound crisper, the rhythm section has more punch, the guitars ring with much more clarity. Reissue producer Steve Hoffman, who is as good sonically as anyone who ever undertook the task, thinks that Dexter had reason to believe that the records as he revamped them sounded better on the phonographs and rather primitive speakers consumers used at the time. Maybe so. They don't now.

In any case, Dexter's changes weren't decisive. By any standard, the overall musical value of both the British and American albums remains immense. What Dexter did was arrogant beyond question, though, and once you know something about Dexter, you're inclined to suspect a passive–aggressive hostility inspired it.

Dexter remained in charge of the Beatles' American album releases from the time he spurned "Love Me Do" through his cockeyed version of *Rubber Soul.* Judging from his decision making on the Beatles, you'd think the man was a rock hater with the A&R judgment of a deaf misanthrope and the engineering skills of a toddler messing with the controls on the family boom box.

But Dexter had been involved in the record business for decades, and he did some good work. In 1944, he produced for Capitol an album called *New American Jazz*. It includes a very fine performance of "Casanova's Lament" that showcases not only a subtle band performance but also one of Jack Teagarden's finer vocals of the period. He made some good early R&B records with the raunchy Kansas City singer Julia Lee. He wrote for *Down Beat* when *Down Beat* was the *Creem Magazine* of jazz, one of the wildest publications of any kind on the newsstand.

But Dave Dexter Jr. loathed rock'n'roll beyond reason. And in print, he comes across as a nasty, vindictive son of a bitch. Eventually, he lived down to the lowest of expectations.

What makes Dex, as he was called by contemporaries, the bad guy isn't just that he passed on the Beatles. Dick Rowe, A&R chief of Decca Records in London, passed too, but at his next opportunity, Rowe signed the Rolling Stones. Dave Dexter Jr. passed on the Beatles at least three separate times, rejecting "Love Me Do," "Please Please Me," and "She Loves You" as having no potential to become hit singles in the United States. The British act he boasted about signing is Freddie and the Dreamers. (I did not make this up.)

In 1988, when he turned over his archives and record collection to the University of Missouri–Kansas City's

Miller Nichols Library, Dexter recorded an oral history with Chuck Haddix. The portion about the Beatles is online at www.umkc.edu/lib/spec-col/dex-bio.htm, and throughout its nine minutes, he is bitterly unrepentant.

The first single, he says, meaning "Love Me Do," "was in with about 17 other sample records. . . . I can only remember that when I heard Lennon playing harmonica on this record, I thought it was the worst thing I'd ever heard. So I nixed it. I didn't want any part of the Beatles."

Dexter then tells the story of the Beatles' sojourns at Vee-Jay and Swan in a version that runs roughly parallel with the truth, except for omitting that he actually got a crack at having Capitol release two more of those discs. As to the Beatles being exiled from EMI's American base, he says, "That was fine with me, 'cause I got hundreds of records from all over the world from all these various EMI companies and we could only put out three a month maybe." It's hard to judge whether equating the Beatles' early singles with *Songs for Sunbathing in Switzerland* and *German Beer-Drinking Music* (one of which Dexter actually boasted of releasing in his book) is more blink-ered or egotistical.

How did the Beatles wind up back at Capitol? Dexter mentions nothing about Sir Joseph Lockwood calling Alan Livingston and reminding him that EMI owned Capitol and that EMI wanted the Beatles' records out in America on Capitol, no matter what kind of benighted jazzbo he had running international A&R. Nothing about

Brian Epstein calling Alan Livingston and pleading with him to give at least one listen to "I Want to Hold Your Hand." (Livingston told Spizer he went "downstairs" to get the company's only copy of the single that Dave Dexter Jr. *had already rejected*.)

No, no. Approval by Capitol for finally releasing a single by England's biggest musical attraction came the only way it could, through the magic ears of the great Dave Dexter Jr., of course.

"In September, I think it was, or maybe October," Dexter continues in his oral history, "I went out on one of my long trips and I spent some time in England. And the A&R man there said, 'Oh, I've got a record I know you're gonna want to issue.' 'Oh, fine, that's why I'm here. Let me hear it.'

"So he puts this 45-rpm single on and I said, 'Who is it?' He said, 'Never mind, never mind.' I said, 'No, tell me. I like to know who I'm listening to.' He said, 'No, let me surprise you.' So he put the needle down and it was 'I Want to Hold Your Hand.'

"And boy, I heard about four bars of that and grabbed it. I knew it was the Beatles. So Capitol recovered the mighty Beatles quartet."

Great story. Trouble is, nobody else ever told the story that way. Every Beatles biography of any repute has Lockwood calling Livingston to break the bottleneck, which consisted of one man, Dave Dexter Jr.

You're welcome to believe Dexter's version, of course.

But you should know more about who Dexter was before choosing sides.

———

Go back to the beginning of Dave Dexter's role in the Beatles affair. Dexter's aversion to the harmonica is peculiar. According to Bruce Spizer, "Having produced several R&B discs for Capitol, Dexter believed that the harmonica was a blues instrument that had no place in pop music." Spizer says the harmonica also determined Dexter's decision not to release "Please Please Me."

At pretty much the same time that he rejected "Love Me Do," he also rejected Frank Ifield's "I Remember You," which featured a harmonica—and became a top-five American hit on Vee-Jay. Only a few months before, Bruce Channel had scored a number-one hit in America with "Hey Baby," on which the lead instrument was Delbert McClinton's harmonica. A folk revival was going on in America, and Capitol had the most important pop-folk group, the Kingston Trio, which sometimes used harmonica and had huge hits.

Hire anybody to find talent and assist the talent in finding material—the function of the A&R (artist and repertoire) person—and you hire blind spots. He or she will always have justifications for why those blind spots reflect good judgment, too. The problem is that the reasons the A&R man offers aren't necessarily what's really going into the decisions.

———

Capitol president Alan Livingston thought it made sense to have Dave Dexter, at that time 48 years old, decide that American pop audiences, mainly teenagers and young adults, didn't want to hear John Lennon's harmonica. He kept thinking this even after the summer of 1963, when Vee-Jay's release of "From Me to You" spent six weeks on the playlist at KRLA, the biggest station in Los Angeles, where Capitol was based. It eventually reached number 42 there, six months before Beatlemania began.

"There was just no interest in English artists here," Livingston told Spizer. "We had no success at all, but because of the relationship [EMI owned Capitol], I felt we had to screen everything they sent us. I couldn't just brush it off, so I gave one of my producers at Capitol the assignment of listening to every EMI record that was sent to us. His name was Dave Dexter. And Dave was a good musicologist, he was a writer, he was a producer, and I trusted Dave's ears and was not concerned about it."

Livingston said this more than 30 years after it became clear that Dave Dexter didn't have a clue about the commercial potential of the Beatles. The statement either amounts to a kind of loyalty one just doesn't find anymore or a complete refusal to grapple with the issue.

Anyway, Dexter didn't have such impeccable ears and he wasn't necessarily all that professional. He turned down Frankie Laine, then the road manager of a popular group, without so much as a listen. Laine became one of the biggest pop singers of the 1940s and 1950s. Dexter had somehow alienated "the intemperate and intransigent" Frank Sinatra.

Dex says he brought Kay Starr to Capitol. ("'She sings with all the bluesy, gut-grabbing verve of Bessie Smith,' I pleaded." Let us pause while those among us who've heard Starr's biggest hit, "The Rock and Roll Waltz," recover from their hysterics.)

Starr was signed to Capitol's country roster, which Dex had nothing to do with. He says he brought Stan Kenton, Nat King Cole, and Peggy Lee to the label. He probably had a role in all of these. He was never important enough to be granted credit, even if he deserved it. It's as likely that he didn't as that he did since, as we shall see, Dexter's regard for facts is selective.

It's hard to know when he's on the square because, beyond his dubious boasts, Dex did have a few hits before the Beatles. He supervised Jerry Leiber and Mike Stoller's production of the seminal rock song "Black Denim Trousers and Motorcycle Boots" by the Cheers, which was a top-10 hit in 1955. His account of Leiber and Stoller at that time is fascinating and amusing, at the end even begrudgingly admiring. His account of later discovering that Edith Piaf had recorded the song is funnier, and more succinct: "To me it seemed like mixing a dill pickle with ice cream. I put it out. It didn't sell."

It had been obvious for a while by then that the kind of jazz and pop Dex loved—the music from before to just after World War II—was no longer commercial. So after Capitol merged with EMI in 1956, he volunteered to supervise international A&R, which meant auditioning releases from EMI branches throughout the British Empire, most of them featuring local music. He says he did it to take advantage of his expertise. "For 15 years I had read the London *Melody Maker* music newspaper every week. My knowledge of British bands and singers was at least a tad better than anyone else's at Capitol."

But really, I think, he just wanted out of what the contemporary American music scene had become. In *Playback,* when he describes his 1950 encounter with the 16-year-old girl from Hollywood High who loved Bullmoose Jackson, he says he remembers the incident "like a painful childhood enema."

"'You have to blame Thomas Alva Edison for today's rock'n'roll. He invented electricity.'—Stan Getz," reads the epigraph to *Playback*'s chapter 12. Later, Dexter remarks, "In time, rock'n'roll took over the market. It became increasingly difficult to sell legitimate music." Straight from the heart of the man who cobbled together the *Help!* "soundtrack" album.

Early in Dexter's international tenure, a single by Laurie London, "He's Got the Whole World in His Hands," made number one, although Dexter acknowledges he had little to do with it. On one of his trips to Europe Dex decided that the US market would accommodate an album called *German Beer-Drinking Music.*

It sold well enough for Capitol to issue a second volume. There were some other slight successes. He claims credit for Ron Goodwin's "Swingin' Sweethearts," which he pulled off a British Goodwin album. It made number 52 at its chart peak.

As for the rest of Dexter's accomplishments while running the international A&R department, it's painful to measure reality against his claims. "I issued dozens of British rock singles, month by month. Cliff Richard was the Presley of England, a handsome young singer who dominated the British charts, but over here we couldn't give his singles away. Nor would American deejays grant him air exposure." He expressly told Chuck Haddix that he'd released numerous singles by Richard. Capitol put out two.

He says that Franck Pourcel's "Only You" became the first French record to sell a million copies in the United States. The record did make the top 10 in 1959, the act billed as Franck Pourcel's French Fiddles. Capitol never had "Only You" certified as a gold record, as it commonly did with big hits; Pourcel never charted an album, and he never charted a follow-up single.

Dexter also writes that the albums he released by British singer Patricia Clark—*In London*, *In Love and In London*, and *In Love Again*—were "popular." No singer named Patricia Clark has ever had a chart record in America.

This documentation would be overkill if not for the

claims Dexter made after he left Capitol about the role he had played with the Beatles, and about the Beatles' supposed gratitude for his work on their albums. He claimed that both McCartney and Lennon thanked him for "improving" the albums.

The reality of Dexter's relationship with the Beatles is closer to the story Bruce Spizer tells about Capitol's rejection of "She Loves You." "[George Martin] remembers getting a curt reply from the company that they did not think the Beatles would do anything in America. The party line out of Capitol was that the Beatles' music 'wasn't suitable for the American market.'"

If you've read *Playback*, that's Dave Dexter, word for word and proud of it.

Dave Dexter Jr. was born in 1915 in Kansas City. His father, Dave Dexter Sr., worked as a sportswriter at the *Kansas City Star*, the city's most important newspaper. By the time Dave Jr. was in high school, he had become a confirmed jazz fan and aspiring newspaperman. But when Dex was 21, he dropped out of the University of Missouri's famous journalism school to take a job at the *Kansas City Journal-Post*. There, he wrote the nothing stories required of an apprentice, but also kept his hand in the entertainment business by covering jazz and other celebrities when they hit town.

Dave Jr. arrived in time to get in practically on the

---

ground floor of jazz in its Kansas City heyday, when it was still beautifully disreputable. Judging by his account in *Playback*, he didn't struggle much to make it more couth, either, although he seems to have done his best to make its vulgarities more acceptable to a wider audience.

He knew pretty much everyone in the Kansas City scene and, thanks to his job at the *Journal-Post*, met key national jazzmen as they passed through. He didn't like them all equally, of course: He found a young alto player named Charles Parker particularly offensive, perhaps because Charlie, not yet nicknamed "Yardbird," nicknamed him "Dexterious," which he found objectionable enough to mention it at least three times in *Playback*. (It reads like me complaining that back in Detroit, Iggy Pop used to call me "Marshmallow.")

Dexter became a stringer for *Down Beat*, the Chicago-based jazz paper that had begun a few years before as a handout for an agent peddling life insurance. It unexpectedly grew into the main organ of the jazz scene and was avidly read each week by musicians from coast to coast. It was one of the most free-swinging magazines in America, a cross between the serious critical writing of *Rolling Stone* and the sensationalist celebrity "reporting" of the *National Enquirer*, minus the UFO stories common to both.

In 1938, *Down Beat* offered Dexter a job as associate editor in its Chicago headquarters and the 23-year-old snapped it up. Mainly, he worked with volunteer stringers collecting the week's news and opinion, but he tells hilarious stories about owner–editor Carl Cons trying to amplify circulation by writing headlines that hung the facts of a story by a thread. One morning, he says, Cons came in and saw Dexter editing the front page. The boss grabbed a pencil and said, "Here's what I want to see in this spot," drawing in pictures of Benny Goodman and Artie Shaw, the two most commercially important bandleaders in the country. Above them, he wrote, "SHAW STABS GOODMAN WITH PARING KNIFE."

"Or it can be vice versa," he said.

Dexter's accounts of his years at *Down Beat* in *Playback* and his 1946 book, *Jazz Cavalcade*, and of *Down Beat*'s role in the jazz world of the late thirties and early forties are engrossing, much more so than anything else he wrote. The lack of contradiction between the two books, written almost 30 years apart, lends me faith that they're at least accurate to his memory.

Dexter held to the *Down Beat* ethic for the rest of his life. His accounts of events around the Beatles can be vastly entertaining simply for the shameless way he lays his tales at right angles to reality. "Our sales and promotion staff didn't know whether to take me [seriously], since I had constantly cried, 'Wolf,' so many times before," he told David Pritchard and Alan Lysaght in *The Beatles: An Oral History*. "I'd tell them how big a hit something was somewhere in Europe or whatever, and they didn't want any more imported records to sell. They were happy enough to sell the Beach Boys, Nat King Cole, and a few others. So without any promotion the Beatles were an absolute phenomenon. By New Year's [1964] the orders for "I Want to Hold Your Hand" were in the millions, and there had been no promotion that first week! The only thing I can remember was that the old Huntley-Brinkley news hour showed a little short [piece] about how hysterical Beatle fans were over in England. That might have caused a little stir, but by the first week of 1964, we were hiring RCA Victor and other record labels to press [discs]."

(A great deal of American publicity about the Beatles was generated in autumn 1963: pieces on NBC's *Huntley-Brinkley Report* and the *CBS Evening News*; Ed Sullivan witnessing Beatlemania at Heathrow Airport in London and booking the group for three appearances on his Sunday-night TV show; articles in *Time* and *Newsweek*; and the advance airplay in Washington, St. Louis, and Chicago. It's true, though, that Capitol's minions had no hand in it. Thanks primarily to Dave Dexter dragging his heels on signing the band, the group was not officially signed to Capitol until December 4.)

"Later, when the Beatles were in Florida, I called them to see if they liked the sound of the Capitol issue—we changed some of the sound characteristics from the British Parlophone record—and they assured me the sound was even better, [that it had] a hotter sound and a little more volume."

In this brief statement, Dexter retails all sorts of whoppers. He implies he had wanted to release the records he rejected; he lays the fault for the lack of response to the Beatles before "I Want to Hold Your Hand" at the foot of the sales and marketing staff; he overstates sales dramatically, since orders for the first single by New Year's 1964 were closing in on one million but not several times that; there had been plenty of promotion, including forcing the poor sales staff all over the country to wear Beatles wigs; the Beatles made it clear many times over, in 1964 and ever since, that they loathed the "sound characteristics" (reverb and EQ) Dexter had added; even to amateur ears, the sound on the Dexterized Beatles records is *less* hot, not more.

This is straight out of the *Down Beat* handbook. "'We must have something sensational in every issue, Dex,'" he writes that Cons told him. "'If it doesn't happen you must make it happen. Call up bandleaders and the top singers. Get them to make wild statements. Feuds are what we want, anything to make bold headlines. . . . We reflect the mores and behavior of the professional musician.'" Of course, under the circumstances, I probably should point out that for all I know, Cons said exactly the opposite to Dexter and what is represented here is a standard he invented for himself. All I can tell you for sure, having read all that he wrote and pretty much everything written about him, is that it was the standard Dave Dexter Jr. lived up to for the rest of his career.

By the time Dex went to work at Capitol during the latter part of World War II, he had edited a magazine with John Hammond; written a load of liner notes and other promotional materials for jazzmen he favored (or who could pay him); gotten to know everybody who mattered in the big band scene; become friends with Benny Goodman, the most hostile man in jazz; won a reputation for weirdness with his standard order of beer and ice cream at jazz niteries; become a regular jazz commentator on New York radio; flunked his draft physical; gotten married; and come to the conclusion that the reason that other humans didn't share his taste was that they were ignorant and, if they resisted his jazz advocacy, that they were inferior specimens of the species.

Capitol hired him to be a staff writer, which meant a lot of hackwork—press releases, perfunctory liner notes, bio handouts for artists he didn't care for. Dexter longed to be an A&R man, which meant in those days a talent scout who spent nights at clubs looking for artists to record, days selecting material and arranging session dates for the artists he signed, and during the sessions performing the functions that are today assigned to record producers.

The results mark Dave Dexter Jr. as one of the two

THE MAN WHO HATED THE BEATLES

most pathetic sad sacks in the Beatles story, second only to Pete Best. He tried to get out of the way of rock'n'roll and it just steamrollered his ass. He proceeded to ask for the infamy he got.

Which isn't entirely fair—not that I'm here to be entirely fair. Whatever Dex started out to be, it wasn't a sad sack. The early photos of him, from the late thirties and the forties, show a young guy—maybe the first professional jazz journalist, maybe an astute hanger-on in the scene—who's just on the square side of hip. He wears the correct high-waisted trousers, his hair is usually perfect. There's a shot of him in *Playback*, taken in 1945. He's in the studio, standing behind Teagarden, making *New American Jazz*. Dex wears a tweed sport coat over a striped crew-neck T-shirt. He looks like he can handle whatever might happen, and he seems to be in his glory working with guys like that, especially on an album that was his concept from start to finish.

You want to like this guy, especially if you admire some of the causes he championed (Woody Herman, Julia Lee, Andy Kirk and His Clouds of Joy) or any of the records he made.

But how does someone who can make "Casanova's Lament," a white man singing the blues if ever a white man did, not understand and welcome the jump-blues synthesis of rock'n'roll? How does he wind up being the guy we see in the pictures from the Beatles era, the guy in the picture in *Playback* where he's posed with California governor Pat Brown? Now Dex has become a stout corporate executive wearing a tweed suit and a white shirt with a skinny black tie. He's got a crew cut and, though he's smiling, the wrinkles around his eyes scream "angry white man."

The journey he took involves the frustration of becoming a cog in a big corporation, which is what Capitol was by the early 1960s; of having great ambitions as a writer, reporter, producer, and talent scout and realizing none of them; of being a parent of teenagers who (he makes clear) rejected his musical taste, which to him meant they sided with the enemy; who's got a history that includes watching *Down Beat* deteriorate, *New American Jazz* flop in the marketplace, and being damaged personally and professionally by Sinatra's refusal to even let him hang around his session; who's steered into a corner at work and reduced to bragging about the sales of the German beer-drinking music album.

———

For me, to see this sour Dave Dexter Jr. is to remember the face of my father.

But though my dad was that angry and that square and, oh yes, that rednecked, he was not vindictive and he prized telling the truth. Dave Dexter was both a nasty spiteful man and, even when it was unnecessary, a guy who evaded the facts. More than that, he was a misanthrope—he just didn't like people very much.

———

THE MAN WHO HATED THE BEATLES

I imagine the last seems the hardest to believe and maybe it does go a little too far. Maybe he just loathed teenagers.

He was, in both New York and Los Angeles, a frequent participant on radio shows where critics rated records. (He must have been good at it, though *Playback* is devoid of interesting comment on actual music.) At one point, the shows in New York became very popular, popular enough to attract a fan base interested in meeting the regulars. Dexter described what happened in his autobiography: "And so for the remainder of my residence in New York, I pondered the aberrational behavior of teenaged girls who waited in the halls and lobbies of WOV and WMCA to scream and shove for autographs of an unpaid ex-Missouri newsman who exited the two studios every Wednesday and Friday evening intent only on finding a seat on the subway home to Queens. But it happened to me, month after month, and it was to occur again after I moved to California during World War II. Who can explain the mental and emotional content of the minds of immature young ladies—and certain young men as well? I won't even try."

Like many misanthropes, Dexter believed himself exceptionally moral. To get the full flavor of Dexter the moralist's relationship to facts, consider this wonderful anecdote, from *Jazz Cavalcade*: "The most hilarious example of a maestro assuming the role of vocalist is recalled in connection with Red Norvo's 1938 discing of 'You Must Have Been a Beautiful Baby.' Mildred Bailey was scheduled to sing the lyric, but she took one brief glance at the lead sheet and balked as only La Belle Mildred can. While the engineers frantically deplored the impasse and the time wasted, Norvo, his wife, and a young baritone who sang with the Norvo orchestra, Terry Allen, suddenly decided to organize a vocal trio on the spot. Without a rehearsal the three gleefully talked their way through an entire 'vocal' chorus while the men in the band were bent over with laughter. Brunswick issued the record a few weeks later with the vocal chorus duly credited to 'The Three Ickies'! Of course the platter has since become a rare collector's item."

Would the story be that much worse if Dexter had acknowledged that Red Norvo's wife was Mildred Bailey?

As to vindictive, his account of Charlie Parker's life, from his 1964 book, *The Jazz Story: From the '90s to the '60s*, conveys a barely conceivable lack of sympathy. "Charlie Parker was a spoiled brat," it began, going on to note that in Kansas City, "he was called a 'mommy's boy' by musicians who quickly tired of his thinking only of Parker." The dialect of the entire chapter, 11 printed pages, is ad hominem. At the end, Dexter comes as close as he dares to acknowledging the music: "Bird's revolutionary playing will live forever, although there were as many musicians who disliked it, didn't understand it, and didn't want to hear any more of it as there were those who called Parker a genius."

But Dex has already had his knife in deep. "There are

some who insist that Parker's suicide attempt [drinking iodine] was an act, and that he merely smeared iodine on his tongue with cotton in September 1954. It gave him admission to New York's public Bellevue Hospital (for the second time) and perhaps a rest and a chance to think things out for two weeks." A beautiful passage to those who admire the poisonous finesse of a tabloid gossip energized by all the petty malice of a man who never forgave a slight ("Dexterious"). Parker has been dead for 50 years. Try and find another source who doubts that his suicide attempts were real.

The man who wrote this swill programmed the American albums by the Beatles from 1964 to 1966.

———

It certainly didn't have to be like that. In Canada, it was almost exactly the opposite, thanks to a Capitol employee named Paul White. White had been a British journalist until he immigrated to Canada in the mid-1950s. He rose in esteem at the Canadian Capitol company when he put together a hit album with the English jazz sax player Freddy Gardner, whose music came to his attention on a tip from a Capitol sales rep who reported some demand for it.

White started by being in charge of catalog compilations—the job to which Dexter sank after he was removed from the international A&R job. Pop singles were soon added to his purview. He found further success

———

in Canada, always more Anglophile than the Lower 48, with English records like "My Boomerang Won't Come Back" by Charlie Drake, Ifield's "I Remember You," and "I Don't Care" by Helen Shapiro, the top of the bill on the Beatles' first national tour back home.

In January 1963, White received a copy of "Love Me Do," which had been released the previous October in the UK. He liked it instantly. "One evening, as I was getting bored again listening to all these 45s, 'Love Me Do' slipped out of its sleeve and plunked down onto the turntable. I thought, 'My God, that's different!' I only thought it was different because, although the guys were definitely singing a simple lyric, they seemed to be happy doing it, compared to the guys on the other 50 records I'd heard that week," he told Bruce Spizer. "So I put them on the 'must listen again' pile." In February, the record was released to whopping Canadian indifference; only a station in London, Ontario, played it on the radio, and the total sales are estimated to have been fewer than 200 copies.

White had Capitol Canada put out "Please Please Me," too. The airplay and sales were about the same.

He put out "From Me to You," despite the fact that Del Shannon, a major star just then, had his own version of the song out. (Shannon had toured with the Beatles in Britain.) The two discs fought it out for airplay from June through July, when Shannon's finally won. The Beatles' "From Me to You" sold about 500 copies in Canada.

When "She Loves You" arrived, the president of Capitol Canada sat Paul White down and asked what he was trying to do. White said he believed in the group. The boss said, "I'll give you one more chance."

"She Loves You," released in late August in England, came out in late September in Canada. By mid-December it was number one at CPFL in London, which alone had played all the Beatles singles. Shortly thereafter, it went to number one on Toronto's CHUM Hit Parade, the most important national chart. By February 1964 it had sold 150,000 units in Canada. It also dragged the previous releases along behind it into the charts.

While Capitol Canada didn't release the *Please Please Me* album, it did release *With the Beatles,* all 14 tracks intact, albeit with an altered front cover and retitled *Beatlemania! With the Beatles.* It was from this release that White pulled out "Roll Over Beethoven," backed it with "Please Mr. Postman," and scored a hit in Canada and the United States. All of this was accomplished by early December 1963 simply because Paul White paid attention, understood what he was hearing, compared it to what was happening in Britain, and kept plugging.

Under Paul White's direction, the Canadian Capitol released hits by such English EMI artists as the Hollies, the Dave Clark 5, the Animals, Herman's Hermits, and the Yardbirds.

In the US, Capitol had first stab at all of these acts and passed *after* the Beatles bottleneck was broken. Its international A&R man refused to release every one of them. And he kept his job until 1966.

———

Maybe Alan Livingston considered Dex a pretty good guy who'd made a mistake, maybe he thought that now that the group was firmly in Capitol's grasp and the biggest act since Elvis, nobody could screw it up. Maybe Livingston didn't really like the Beatles any more than Dave Dexter and his own wife (a B-list actress whose response to hearing "I Want to Hold Your Hand" was "Are you kidding?"). A 1966 memo from Dex to Livingston in the Dexter archives reportedly responds to Livingston's idea that there should be an all-McCartney concept album ("Michelle" and "Yesterday" on the same platter might have made zillions). Dex sensibly advises against this.

Or maybe, and this would have been true enough before January 1964, Livingston just didn't think of the album market as that important for rock'n'roll. But the Beatles changed that, too. In fact you could argue that the biggest immediate change they wrought was converting rock'n'roll from a singles market to an album market. (It took the Internet to change it back again, and the Beatles were until 2007 the biggest holdouts on making their material available for download.)

Meet the Beatles outsold any of the Beatles' singles— no rock act, not even Elvis, had ever made an album that outsold its hits. In the long-term, the profit implications for record companies were immense, especially if the companies could milk the material as Capitol did with the Beatles, the flagship not only of their artist roster but of the industry.

Dave Dexter Jr. made a hell of a milkman as he rummaged through available Beatles releases, picking off stray tracks here and there from singles, EPs, previous albums, upcoming albums. On *Beatles '65*, maybe he did deserve producer credit. There is no album quite like it in the Beatles catalog anywhere else in the world. (And I like that one, too, although I don't cherish it.) On *Help!* the credit reads more like blame if you know that Dexter put it together during a studio all-nighter, collecting snippets of orchestral score and adding the Beatles songs from the movie—his bitching and moaning reaches its approximate peak in this section of *Playback*. He claimed that George Martin told him there would be no *Help!* soundtrack album.

Despite Dexter's contention, there *was* a British album called *Help!* But it's not a soundtrack. Did George Martin deliberately mislead Dexter?

The British *Help!* has seven tracks in common with the United States release of the same title. The British album does not have "In the Tyrol" by Richard Wagner or an instrumental called "Another Hard Day's Night," or "James Bond Theme," another instrumental. The US version has all those and a couple of other instrumentals, too. The Beatles don't play on any of the instrumentals.

Where is the missing material from the UK *Help!*?

Dexter had already used "You Like Me Too Much," "Tell Me What You See," and "Dizzy Miss Lizzy" on *Beatles VI*, released two months earlier. "Yesterday" and "Act Naturally" appeared on the infamous *Yesterday . . . and Today* some months later, the last of the Dexterized albums—but not Dexterized by Dexter, who'd been demoted to (in his own words) "a job without a title," compiling old records for a licensee who sold them at rock-bottom prices in grocery stores and five-and-tens.

"I've Just Seen a Face" and "It's Only Love" Dexter whacked into the midst of *Rubber Soul* (the former became that album's lead track!), meaning that four, not three, songs were dropped from the British *Rubber Soul*, and if that album's song sequence and selection are not intentional and aesthetically important, you can take "Louie Louie" and cram it into *Porgy and Bess* without apology. (Four, not five, because Capitol allowed the Beatles 12 tracks on that album, as it did for such worthies as the Lettermen. Good sense prevailed, however, and the even more intricately conceived 14-track *Revolver* was released in America with only 11 tracks, with the remainder appearing on *Yesterday . . . and Today*.)

Yesterday . . . and Today was the end of Dexterization because the Beatles had (whether they'll admit it or not) served notice on how much they hated Capitol's (to be fair, let's call it Capitol's) hackwork by submitting for the cover a photograph of the band wearing butcher's smocks and holding bloody raw meat and equally bloodied limbs and torsos from dismembered baby dolls. The cover got banned, but it was the last time Capitol carved up the Beatles' catalog.

But had the Beatles and Beatles fans really faced their last Dexterization? They had not. John Lennon's obituary was yet to come.

"There's Dave Dexter, a thirty-year man at Capitol until he was given six-weeks' notice in 1974," wrote Arnold Shaw in his R&B history, *Honkers and Shouters*. It's hard to see Dexter as much of a victim, although 59 is young to be fired from a job you've held since you were in your twenties. Still, Dex held on to his job for more than a decade past the worst piece of judgment in music industry history. He held the "job with no title" for eight years. About a year after he left, *Billboard*, the music industry's leading trade publication, published his autobiography.

Dexter wound up going to work at *Billboard* as a copy editor and grumpy old man, still convinced the music had gone to shit and deeply dismayed by the hairy, licentious, dope-smoking generation of musicians who were not his own.

On December 8, 1980, John Lennon was assassinated on his doorstep in New York City by a Christian zealot. Lennon had just released his first solo album in five years, *Double Fantasy*, with Yoko Ono. It was a fine album, and John acted as proud of it as he had the right to be. He was visible again and talking as avidly and interestingly as ever about music and events. Then . . . gone. The entire world went into shock.

Billboard prepared a series of special Lennon stories for its issue dated December 20. All but one of the articles praised Lennon for his musical, political, and personal achievements; for his courage, insight, and wit; for daring to toss over his stardom in order to involve himself intensely in raising his son Sean.

The other article was written by Dave Dexter Jr.

"Nobody's Perfect" read the bar over the headline: "Lennon's Ego & Intransigence Irritated Those Who Knew Him." Datelined "Los Angeles," it began, "No pop artist since the early 1960s was more musically gifted than John Lennon.

"And of the four Beatles, Lennon was—among those in the industry who worked with him—the most disliked."

Dexter recounted what he called Lennon's and the Beatles' failures—mainly it came down to the early singles flopping and the band's breaking up when there was still money on the table. He didn't mention his own role until the middle of the piece, when he wrote that "When enough tapes arrived from England we spent hours adjusting the British Parlophone equalization and adding reverb to conform to Capitol's standards." He repeats his fantastical claim that McCartney called from Miami to praise the sound quality; this time, John was on the line, too.

Later, though, Dexter had been personally betrayed by

the Beatles. "Lennon advised Capitol's management that he didn't care for the album covers Capitol was devising. Lennon didn't like the back covers, either. Nor did he approve the sounds of the Beatles tapes issued by Capitol, an abrupt 180-degree turnaround from his previous praise. . . . McCartney, George Harrison and Ringo Starr did not complain. Only Lennon."

He recounted his story of the cocktail party at Alan Livingston's house before the Hollywood Bowl concert in 1964, when Lennon allegedly said of some autograph-seeking neighborhood kids, "Why those bloody little bastards, they try to interfere with us constantly, try to deprive us of our privacy. We've had it with 'em, mate."

Then back to Lennon's foibles: He demanded a different manager than the others (actually, that was Paul). He differed violently over Apple's management (there is no record of any such difference, let alone a violent one). "And it was Lennon who bitched the loudest about my choice of songs to be included in the group's Capitol albums," says Dexter. "Loudest" is an interesting comment given that he's just claimed there were no other complainers. You'd think John called him Dexterious.

It was classic gutter journalism. Begin with nonspecific praise; continue with innuendo, half-truth, and outright lies; conclude the damning passages with a faux "explanation" that in fact throws further grime into the mix—in this case, "His abnormal childhood made him an abnormal adult." Then end with a benediction that is itself littered with hostility: "Lennon will be remembered well for his musical contributions. Unlike himself there was nothing eccentric or unlikable about John's artistry. And that's what all of us will remember."

All but one.

Nobody who knew Dexter could have been surprised by this outburst of spleen, but it was shocking that *Billboard* printed it, not so much because the magazine never published anything hostile about anyone (although in those days it didn't), but because it was so obviously a bitter attack from a failed hanger-on.

It was also stupid. At the time of his death, Lennon was signed to Geffen Records. David Geffen was the most powerful man in the music industry and you ain't seen merciless 'til you've watched him conduct a feud. Geffen called for an industry-wide advertising boycott of *Billboard*, and there was a good deal of compliance, even after the next issue printed a rebuttal commentary by Alan Livingston and several furious letters from others who knew Lennon.

I don't know if Dexter got fired. Once again, he deserved to be.

But then, look at it this way: John Lennon lived 40 years and created music that will last forever. It is very likely that Dave Dexter Jr., who lived almost twice as many years, will be forgotten as soon as you finish this book and resume listening to the Beatles records he was too shallow and narrow-minded to appreciate.

8

BUILDING COMPLEXITY
OUT OF SIMPLICITY

There's a faint hint of order in the sequencing of the five Lennon–McCartney originals on *The Beatles' Second Album*, though given the randomness of Dexterization that's probably accidental. But these five originals give a very exact reading of why the Beatles took the world by storm in 1963 and 1964, just as the material the Beatles didn't create from scratch contains a wealth of information about where they came from and what their original ambitions were. There is even an important foreshadowing of the band's future—Lennon's portion of that future, of course, since none of the originals features a McCartney lead vocal.

Most of these original songs are orphans, cast off as B sides or minor UK album tracks. In a way that's one of the virtues of the *Second Album*, the way it brings to light recordings that were simply lost—overshadowed, to tell the truth—on the British albums, and weren't *something* enough to be singles. You have to be nonspecific about what the *something* was, since one of them, "I Call Your Name," was a single for Billy J. Kramer and the Dakotas and later such a well-known album track for the Mamas and the Papas that they included it on their *Greatest Hits*.

Two of the B sides, "You Can't Do That" and "Thank You Girl," charted in the early months of 1964 as the flip sides of "Can't Buy Me Love" and "Do You Want to Know a Secret," respectively. At that time, virtually any record the Beatles made would receive enough airplay to make the *Billboard* lists. To me, it's as weird that "I'll Get You" didn't chart along with "She Loves You" as that "I Want to Hold Your Hand" made number one and "I Saw Her Standing There" failed to crack the top 10. It was the early days and there was such an abundance of great music pouring out of the Beatles that anomaly became common.

That such a thing could happen also speaks to the incredibly high quality of every track the Beatles recorded in those first months. Okay, I could do without Paul's show tunes, true, but those were tossed in like favors for an aged but doting aunt or Brian Epstein. As I said earlier, they didn't count. The songs that did count were beautiful, powerful, singular, revelatory—the difference between the best and the worst is a matter of nothing more than degree.

"Thank You Girl" blares to life with a mighty blast from John's harmonica—it's meant as an assault, and that's certainly how Dexter would have heard it. I prefer to think of it as a Liverpudlian ram's horn, defined in my dictionary as "a means of making important announcements, rallying the forces to battle and proclaiming the coronation of kings." It said all these things and more to me.

Which is a way of saying that "Thank You Girl" is worth talking about only as a performance. The song itself is nothing—a token of appreciation to some unidentifiable lass, interchangeable with a thousand others in a thousand times that many songs. It's the kind of hackwork that used to flood out of 1650 Broadway to serve as fodder for Elvis albums and girl-group B sides. It doesn't really come up to that standard, since it contains clichés so hoary it's amazing that Martin let John and Paul get away with them. They jump into the corn right from the start: "You've been good to me, you made me glad when I was blue / And eternally, I'll always be in love with you"—as shamelessly banal as anything in McCartney's later catalog of silly love songs, but not to be pinned on poor Paul, not with John taking the lead with such bravado.

But the Beatles were crafty, too. The greeting card couplet features 12 open vowels—"You've," "to," "me," "you," "made," "me" again, "blue," "eternally" (one at each end), "always," "be" again, and "you" at the end. This carries through in the rest of the song, in phrases like "too good to be true," "a thing or two," "only a fool," and of course, "all I've gotta dooooooo" just before the title is sung, the title with its bell-ringing "you" in the middle. There's nothing arch about it—in a way, the banality of the words gives it conversational credibility, it sounds like the sort of stuff an on-the-make (shamelessly on-the-make) lad might have spouted in precoital hope or postcoital delirium.

What's wonderful is how well the song sings, how it's built to do that (that gorgeous flow from the unison "You've been good to me . . ." line into the John and Paul harmony with "And eternally . . .") and how the Beatles ask nothing more of it or themselves. Ringo's back there rockin', of course, at times he sounds like he's going to bang the door off its hinges, then he lays back until his beautiful little set of fills toward the end. Ringo sounds to me on the *Second Album* like the most accomplished musician in the band, both the steadiest and the most imaginative. (That's one reason Paul's pushing him around in the *Let It Be* film inspired revolt not only from Ringo but from fans. He's never let *us* down, one wants to tell McCartney.) For these two minutes, the quintessential guitar-bass-and-drums band becomes a great harmonica-and-drums quartet with the stringed instruments hanging around for additional percussive drive.

At the start of "You Can't Do That," George brings out his 12-string Rickenbacker, which sounds as close to a piano as a guitar can get, but he's interrupted by Paul bashing a cowbell and Ringo, busy with a set of bongos. Amidst this turmoil, John enters with an almost charmless vocal meant to be tough but so flat-footed that it just sounds mean—and not a little desperate. Lennon knew something about jealousy, and as the lyric goes on and on about what this girl cannot do, what becomes more and more apparent is that she can, and she is, and she very well may continue. John knows how toothless all his threats are, too: "But if they'd seen you talking that way, they'd laugh in my face." The invulnerable Wilson Pickett is supposed to be John's model here, but I don't buy it for a second.

There is redemptive power in the harmonies and vocal responses—when the other voices finally arrive at the end of the second verse, they're audibly holding him up, long enough to get those open-throated vowels again ("green," "seen"). Then comes the bridge, where John takes a crack at a Little Richard–style scream, then barges into a bright and nasty little guitar solo that might be the only reason the girl hung around enduring his harangue. This is guitar smashing in a different mode—while the physical instrument survives, Lennon absolutely shreds the music, stomps it, puts into it all the rage at (forget the girl's superficial infidelity, the criminal act of speaking with another guy) his own impotence. You don't have to be a teenage boy to fully appreciate this, but it helps. And I suppose you could take that furious, almost awkward, snarling guitar solo as Lennon's reminder that once you've been one, you're never going to forget the experience. (It can be argued, not inaccurately in my experience, that you're never going to stop being a teenage boy at some levels—in case you've wondered how antique rock'n'rollers persist without reform.)

"I Call Your Name" emerged from a deeper remembrance of adolescent anguish. "That was my song," Lennon said of it. "When there was no Beatles and no group, I just had it around. It was my effort as a kind of blues originally, and then I wrote the middle eight just to stick it in the album when it came out years later. The first part had been written before Hamburg even. It was one of my *first* attempts at a song." As such, it's hard not to imagine that the woman the singer sits and pines over in the darkness is not his lover but John's mother, Julia, killed by a passing car when he was in his teens. It's an obvious reading, though not one that would have been guessed at in 1964.

At the top of the song, the cowbell's back again, clicking away like a late-night clock, as it continues to do throughout the track. But the other voice that matters in "I Call Your Name" is George's Rickenbacker, answering Lennon's strongest imprecations and then taking off on a solo that's based in ska, it's said, but to my ear manages to be jazzy and rockabilly at the same time, before picking up the ticking motif beneath the painful bridge.

"I'm not gonna make it," howls John, and worst of all, "I'm not that kinda man."

BUILDING COMPLEXITY OUT OF SIMPLICITY

In those two minutes, he goes from the aspiring lyricism of an adolescent to the cold sweat realism of the kind of man he will be. He goes from the unwilling confessions of the jealous jerk in "You Can't Do That" to someone who's outgrown his art school pretensions and despite that, finds himself trying to cope with a three o'clock in the morning of the soul. Even the short Little Richard "wooo" on the fade-out can't turn this into *simple* rock'n'roll—it's not rocking but simplicity that has vanished.

Billy J. Kramer's version of "I Call Your Name," the B side of his insipid hit (also written by Lennon–McCartney) "Bad to Me," was not better, but it had two features Lennon liked and he took them for the intro and the genesis of the solo on the Beatles' recording.

The Beatles tossed their version away, slipping it onto the *Long Tall Sally* EP with three oldies, the title cut, Larry Williams's "Slow Down," and "Matchbox," which they got from Carl Perkins and Perkins got from Blind Lemon Jefferson.

"I Call Your Name" is not just the newest but also the most modern song on the album; it hadn't even been released in England when *The Beatles' Second Album* came out. Dexter probably had been sent the parts for the EP and immediately began scavenging it, saving the other two *Long Tall Sally* tracks for *Beatles '65*.

Still, "I Call Your Name" is the one track on the *Sec-*

ond Album that points the way forward—not only in Lennon's lyrical concerns but in the unusual arrangement, particularly the readiness to dare that strange guitar solo.

———

"I'll Get You" is not the future but very much part of that present in which, as McCartney put it to Mark Lewisohn, "we wrote for our market. . . . So a lot of our songs . . . were directly addressed to the fans." He emphasized the use of personal pronouns—I, me, you, your—and in truth, it's hard to think of early Beatles songs without one in the title. "I'll Get You" wins the prize, having such a pronoun both fore and aft.

The pronouns, though, are just what make the lyric of "I'll Get You" a little sinister. The Beatles recorded the song under its working title, "Get You in the End," which wouldn't have helped with that problem. Which is that the singer becomes a stalker. Lennon remains the tough guy and saying he'll get you clearly means he'll fuck you (but only 'cause he loves you). But he's also saying he won't take no for an answer.

My response to that is truly anachronistic. It's not how I thought in 1964, and I don't think the idea of date rape had any currency then. Certainly stalkers and date rapists were not unheard of, but what's now creepy about Lennon as stalker is, among other things, the way he died.

That exemplifies why lyrics should never be disconnected from their musical context. John's singing throughout "I'll Get You" is very gentle, and he doesn't sound truly desperate—he's pleading and there's no hint of false bravado, only real conviction. I trust the respectfully beseeching tone of his singing far more than I trust anything I said in the previous two paragraphs.

The music reemphasizes this. Lennon's harmonica sounds gentler than it ever has before, almost sonorous instead of its usual savage screech. (I know exactly what Dexter didn't like about the way Lennon played harmonica; that doesn't mean he was right.) They're not bashing their guitars this time, just strumming them; Paul's bass is at its most melodic; the handclaps at the beginning are straight off a girl-group hit. I wish Ringo hadn't picked up the beat of the claps on his hi-hat and remained on it for the entirety of the song, but the little fill when he initially comes in is perfection.

The vocal—Lennon by himself or in unison with Paul—picks up all the nuances a reading would miss: "Many, manymany times before" is how he sings it, though on the page it'd be five separate words. It doesn't even matter that at one point, John and Paul seem at odds about which verse they're in. And that refusal to surrender? It soars, as Lennon's voice follows the melody's steps up from "There's gonna be a time" through "I'm gonna change your mind."

The song's refrain seems to be the title phrase, but it's

really "Oh yeah, oh yeah," repeated at the end of each verse, at the beginning of the record, and then two and a half times at the end of the track. "'I'll Get You,'" Tim Riley writes in his Beatles companion, *Tell Me Why*, "counts among the best neglected songs the Beatles ever recorded," and he's right.

———

There's something else about "I'll Get You," a quality it shares with "She Loves You," the A side of the single, which was the Beatles' first million-seller at home and eventually made number one in the States. Both songs were recorded on the same day, July 1, 1963, at Abbey Road. The recording personnel (George Martin and his engineers, Norman Smith and Geoff Emerick) were the same. In the picture taken outside Abbey Road, they all look the same, and they're even all dressed the same, in shirts with collar pins and drainpipe trousers, black boots and skinny ties. John wears a sport jacket.

Maybe everybody was particularly in synch that day— such things happen with performers, as anyone who sees a lot of shows by the same artist will know. But you don't have to know what caused it to note that there's a fullness to the sound, a deep coherence of the musical energy down to its atoms and out to the stars. For the first time, the Beatles sound lush, even in Dexter's mixes, building complexity out of simplicity á la Phil Spector but doing it with an even more rudimentary toolkit—on these songs, there aren't even maracas or a cowbell, let alone a piano, just the bare bones of a rock band, two guitars, bass, and drums.

If "I'll Get You" is the best neglected song the Beatles ever made, "She Loves You" gets my vote as the best single they recorded. While it's playing, it might be the best record ever made. And I mean from Ringo's first drum roll through the exuberance of the first "yeah, yeah, yeah" and the Little Richard "wooo" that finally reaches apotheosis by being repeated, almost giddily, at the beginning of each "yeah, yeah, yeah" refrain after the first. The guitars ring until the end of the verses when George, back on his old reliable six-string Gretsch, gets a resoundingly gritty grind going on. The hi-hat is all over the place again—until they hit the refrain, when it drops out and you hear Ringo at work, busily driving the band toward George's grunting riff.

The lyric is a neat piece of writing—in the first person but addressed to a third. I once mentioned how much I loved this to Beatles publicist Derek Taylor and he stroked his chin while contemplating this encomium, then said avidly, "Yes. Reported dialogue. A tribute to the quality of English grammar schools." In any event, such dialogue is not quite unique among rock lyrics of that time (there's "My Boyfriend's Back," for instance), but it's rare enough.

What makes it more unusual is that Lennon and

McCartney, singing not so much a shared lead but as one voice, not only offer advice but speak as the girl's advocate. They're the voice she hasn't found for herself, the ones who can tell the things she can't or won't. That she has been terribly hurt, but thinks he was acting out of character. That she is not too proud to say she wants him back. But most of all, that she loves him—and they believe her, boy do they ever. It's with this acknowledgement of love that "yeah, yeah, yeah" erupts out of the "wooo" so enthusiastically that you have to wonder what has left the Beatles so giddy. Merely the fact that someone else has fallen in love? I think, rather, that the Beatles never thought there was anything mere about falling in love. After all, at the end of the video anthology, Ringo says, "In the end, it was about four people who loved each other."

I would add that they loved just as much the music in all its majestic simplicity. I don't think you can hear the echo of "Roll Over Beethoven" in "She Loves You," but you can hear a band that understands its spirit. And in the affectionate but sober advice of the final verse ("Pride can hurt you too / Apologize to her"), they also grasp its complications, the idea that sensual pursuit works only in the right context, what their peers in the civil rights movement were calling "the beloved community." In this respect, "She Loves You" is not only the Beatles record that best seizes the moment of Beatlemania (in both Britain and America, six months apart) but points the way to the core of what they'll have to say for the rest of their careers.

"She Loves You" also epitomizes their early singing. For me, it is those vocals that define the Beatles. There are better guitarists than Harrison (not many), more adept drummers than Ringo (fewer still), and better bassists than McCartney (even fewer). Lennon's is one definition of rhythm guitar and he could stomp out a mean solo when he wanted to; he proves that in "You Can't Do That." The Beatles were not at any point, including the heyday of Beatlemania, just another band.

But what floors me, every time, even when I'm not listening for it specifically, is the singing, the joy they put into it, the care they take, the fulsomeness of some of the early harmony and the starkness of some of the leads (in the realm of the raw and the cooked, the *Second Album* is unmistakably raw), the way they make the plain beautiful and bring the complex within reach.

When I think of the origins of "She Loves You," I do not think of Paul and John sitting on twin beds in a tiny Newcastle hotel room, trying to think of rhyming words or chord sequences. I think of them beginning to sing, to tell the story not with words but in their voices, in the way they find to play with words like "glad," to quaver through the last syllable in the second and fourth line of the verses—"daaaay," "saaay," "miiind," "kiiiind," "faiiir," and finally, "her-er-er," which blows the whole thing and they know it, and they know it doesn't matter, it's a kick, a surprise. And then they decide that words like "bad" and "glad" can be stretched, too, and they fill out the chorus with them; it's just a chance to vocalize but they don't want to be Phoebe Snow, they want to be the Beatles, so they do it together and then it's not showing off so much as it is just getting through to the exuberance, the delight they feel about life and how happy they are that they're so good at it. And Paul does his "wooo!" and John responds, in his usual sarcastic fashion, "yeah, yeah, yeah," and then one of them sings it straight, and then they take it from there.

Or maybe it happened at rehearsal or maybe they had "yeah, yeah, yeah" and built that song around it. (No, they didn't.) The thing is, "She Loves You" is their toy, a little game they play with sound. So when they play it for George Martin a little later, after they've rehearsed it enough to figure out that sixth chord they want to end with, and he says it's a terrific number but the ending has to go because it's way too Andrews Sisters, too Glenn Miller (too corny), they try it without. And try it more than once. Martin sees their point, and they get back what they put in and now they are truly glad.

That's how a session like that could take off, could soar, could take something slight and turn it into a sound that rang around the world. "Yeah, yeah, yeah" was not a sarcastic nothing. It was not just the Beatles declaring how happy they were that the world accepted them (John Lennon *grateful*?). It was nothing so simple. It was a taunt, and a challenge, a dare. Critics make a lot of the ability of the artist to say no to so many things (and artists do), but they tend to overlook the power of saying yes. They miss the defiance in it and the daring.

Yeah to three chords. Yeah to slang. Yeah to teenage love affairs, and yeah to trusting your friends to carry the message, and yeah to trusting your other friends to hear it—there are three *yeah*s that every early sixties intellectual (and too many today) would have greeted with a sneer. There are three *yeah*s that could melt a 14-year-old's heart, charge his brain, her spine.

And, 43 years later, you can barely begin to imagine how deeply you will know that can't be bad.

9

MILLIONS OF "YEAH"

What is the measure of greatness for a record album?

In purely artistic terms, it is the quality of the music, and the peripheral things like mixing and mastering that enhance the musical quality. *The Beatles' Second Album* unquestionably falls short on this periphery, even if you believe that the music more than compensates.

But the idea that art exists for its own sake is ludicrous, a gigantic waste of the intellectual effort it takes to sustain the illusion. I understand perfectly well why it arose, as a counter to the idea that art's function is to be propaganda, but countering bullshit with bullshit is a stupid strategy.

One additional measure that always needs to be taken into account is what the album—and not just the album, of course, but any art object—does to and for the people who experience it. What it adds to our lives, what it protects us from, what it exposes us to, what impossibilities it brings to life, what fears it lays to rest. Where it leads us, what dead ends it saves us from pursuing. What joy it brings to dark days, what shades it adds to sunny superficialities. How it teaches us to pursue our own stories, songs . . . lives.

You may think that having this last happen because you listened to "She Loves You," "Long Tall Sally," "I Call Your Name," and "Money" is ridiculous. Maybe it is. Nevertheless, it's what happened.

The Beatles' Second Album is a glorious exposition of the Beatles in 1964: their past, their present, and their future. It also provided some of us with a glimpse of our own future.

That's not exactly why I wanted to write a book about the *Second Album*. I did that because it told a story I wanted, maybe needed, to tell, which is probably the only good reason available. That story is mostly about the music industry and how it works, and fails to work. It's also about the way that genius and stupidity interact. (Thank whatever gods there are, then, for Dave Dexter Jr., for what good story lacks a villain?)

Another part of that story was about me, and what shaped my view of rock'n'roll, the music I've written about—listened to, studied, and defended—for a lifetime, and how I and the music connect to the rest of the world.

The Beatles' Second Album became my favorite because, of course, it confirmed my preconceptions, which were that rock'n'roll at its best possesses and nurtures an intense connection to black popular vocal music and that all music serves its highest function as a means of expressing identity, both individual and collective.

In the end, it's the collective aspect that touches me most deeply. Individualism is a cheap commodity in America, because there's always a surplus of it. Finding some sort of community is a much more difficult task.

The Beatles, bobbing their heads and shouting "yeah!" provided millions of us with both an example of a small group that worked—Ringo's "four people who loved each other"—and a connection to a much larger group consisting of all the millions who assented to that "yeah." Not a small thing, not because it was the sixties and big things were boring, but because we were teenagers, most of us, and your teens are a lonely time of life, a time of not-quite-shared secrets and frightfully open vulnerabilities. The songs on *The Beatles' Second Album* not only speak to that sense of secrets and vulnerabilities, they hint that there are ways out. I guess if you believe that what John Lennon wanted was money, it wouldn't work like that. Roll over, curmudgeon.

The usual thing to talk about when speaking about the Beatles is innocence, but they didn't strike me as innocent at all. They knew lots of things I hadn't figured out yet—listen to "Devil in Her Heart," "I Call Your Name," and "You Really Got a Hold On Me," if you need examples. They knew some things I still can hardly believe are true. One of them is the simple power of music and love to create hope.

This brings me back to "She Loves You." Maybe the Beatles sound innocent because when they chant that initial "She loves you, yeah, yeah, yeah," they unmistakably believe it so firmly. But even to someone who believes as firmly as I do (and always did) that "love is all you need" is a lie, the inescapable truth is that we all do need love. The story of the Beatles, long before the big ambitions took over, involved filling that need and making a generation believe that we could it fill it for ourselves. They told us true.

And for that we should indeed be glad.

Yeah, yeah, yeah.

Yeah, yeah, yeah.

Yeah.

ACKNOWLEDGMENTS

Last night, I worked late reading a friend's commentary on this text, then went to bed and awoke early but refreshed, not least because Beatles songs had filled the soundtrack of all my dreams.

In my experience, such phenomena occur at the beginning of the writing process, when the subject is fresh and you're eager for more, not at the end, when you want mostly to stop worrying about commas, data, and discographies—not to mention your subject matter. Nevertheless, I was more pleased than surprised by the soundtrack. The durability of the Beatles surpasses pretty much any other music I know. And as much as it belongs to the waking world, it belongs to dreams.

It's not part of the *Second Album* but for me, the Beatles record that hums under all of their work—not my favorite song, possibly not even in my top ten, just the one that always speaks to me when I ponder the streamlined beauty of their rock'n'roll—is "Do You Want to Know a Secret."

In "Do You Want to Know a Secret," the Beatles begin with a single word: "Listen."

Listen. There's only so much that words can do. But they can urge.

Listen. Pay attention.

Listen. The first commandment.

The Beatles go on to attempt to extract from each listener a foolish pledge: "Do you promise not to tell?"

But the secrets the Beatles shared had to be told—in a way, sharing the secret *was* the secret.

The secret is, when you find such joy as this, it makes you feel not alone with your dreams but as if the entire world wants to join in. Indeed, in the moment when the Beatles' sounds first reached us, it made our dreams seem as real, sometimes more real, than things much closer and more tangible.

Half of this book is about the songs, one by one. The songs use such rudimentary musical elements, the basics of rock'n'roll, that it might seem you'd have to strain to get much out them. I found no strain, though lots to preoccupy me. If the sounds they make on the *Second Album* are quotidian—two guitars, bass, drums, some weird older guy on piano—what they add up to is not everyday in any sense.

The other half of the book is about voices. It's about the Beatles singing, and the utter pleasure they take in it. There are two voices, and three, and four, and there is one. Sometimes, the two, three, and four are also one and this is not a paradox but so obvious that it's hard to take note of it. It's no less important for being hidden in its own elegance.

ACKNOWLEDGMENTS

The voices that the Beatles raised in song are matched by the lost voices they raised, voices from a rock'n'roll past and present that they resurrected, even though some of those voices were already there, speaking plainly to those who would hear. That circles back to the voices that answered to the Beatles' voices—our voices, by which I don't mean just the thousands who took up amplifiers and microphones in response to them but everyone who found that the Beatles spoke their heart's language. I especially mean those who raised their voices in defense of the pleasure and harmony the Beatles came to symbolize.

Maybe we would have found our voices anyway. But the Beatles set such a fine example of how to use those voices, how to fight with them and how to love with them and how to answer back with cheeky wit rather than a snarl. My generation's sense of humor was defined by Beatles press conferences more than any comedian—even Bob Dylan when he clowned at his press conferences drew on what they'd done.

So these acknowledgments must begin. Without the Beatles, I am something, as are you. With them, we have the chance to be something better. The least I should be is grateful.

I am also grateful to my editor, Pete Fornatale, who came up with the idea not just for me to write a book in this series but to get me to write about the Beatles. I knew exactly what I wanted to do as soon as he said it, and to his credit, he never flinched. Pete was also unfailingly encouraging, never panicky about my bugaboo with deadlines, and did a sensitive and insightful edit. Nancy N. Bailey, project editor, and Nancy Elgin, copy editor, also assisted the way as the best line editors, paying attention to every detail—they are among the best I have worked with.

However, I do believe that on the contract for this book it says the topic is *The White Album*. I took it to be a joke between the two of us and my indispensable agent and friend, Sandra Choron. Sandy's place in my life remains one of its grounding fundamentals. I have now thanked her in something like 25 books, not once adequately. If they invent new words of praise, maybe I'll get it right next time.

Many of my friends responded with enthusiastic encouragement and solid advice. Holly Cara Price, who helped me get started on the research, also gave me a nifty shopping bag made from *Second Album* covers. It's almost as good as she is. Thom Duffy, another friend for more than three decades, provided some crucial information for the Dexter chapter. I mention John Sinclair and Greil Marcus in the text as enthusiasts of the idea; I must add Marta Renzi, who said the *Second Album* was her favorite to dance to, which I believe is about the highest praise she could offer.

Marta's husband, Daniel Wolff, provided more than encouragement—he is my sounding board and we hashed over pretty much every idea and tale in the text at one point or another. I have never had a better friend.

Some of the ideas here were generated when I wrote a

short piece for *Mojo* magazine several years ago about the Beatles arrival in America. I thank those whom I interviewed for it—Al Kooper, Marshall Crenshaw, Mitch Ryder, Nils Lofgren, Sam Moore, Wayne Kramer. *Mojo*'s editors also deserve thanks, in part for keeping the quality of music writing at a high level in general.

Other friends also contributed with dialogue about the Beatles over the years—I am thinking especially of Debbie Geller and Vivek Tiwary but also Harry Choron, John Swenson, and the late Paul Nelson. Special thanks to Barbara Hall and her daughter, Faith Harding, whose Beatlemania and serious musical scholarship beginning at age five remains an inspiration.

One advantage of the age of electronics is that it is much less cumbersome to transmit your work to friends who may be generous enough to read it and help improve it. In this case, I was encouraged—even egged on—by our entire Stratlist e-mail group and improved by notes from Daniel Wolff, Danny Alexander, C. J. Janovy, and most of all, Matt Orel. This book is dedicated to him because although I think he still believes I'm operating from a number of shaky premises, Matt worked damned near as hard as I did, arguing through points, catching mistakes, redoing my math, and serving as my perfect foil, a Beatles fan of the next generation after the British Invasion. Sparring partner, indeed.

As always, thanks to the home front—my wife, Barbara Carr, my daughters, Sasha Carr and Kristen Carr. Can I have the Red and Blue albums back now, kids?

DISCOGRAPHY

THE DEXTERIZED BEATLES ALBUMS

MEET THE BEATLES

Programmed, remixed, and mastered by Dave Dexter. This is primarily material from the UK album, *With the Beatles*.

THE BEATLES' SECOND ALBUM

Programmed, remixed, and mastered by Dave Dexter

SOMETHING NEW

Programmed, remixed, and mastered by Dave Dexter. The process reaches one kind of nadir here, thanks to the inclusion of "Komm, Gib Meir Dein Hand," which is "I Want to Hold Your Hand" sung in German (and intended for release only in German-speaking countries).

BEATLES' '65

Programmed, remixed, and mastered by Dexter

THE EARLY BEATLES

In essence, the material that Dave Dexter had spurned in his job as Capitol's international A&R man. A comparison of how the sound on any of these tracks, all pre-"I Want To Hold Your Hand," to even the VeeJay masters will show exactly what Dexterization consists of.

BEATLES VI

Programmed, remixed, and mastered by Dexter

HELP!

Not only programmed, remixed, and mastered by Dexter but assembled by him from the reels used for the film score. Titles written by Dexter. Completed in one all-nighter and, like any term paper written in that fashion, it shows. Does contain several actual Beatles recordings, however, this does not stop it from being the pits of Capitol's treachery. Many fans, not excluding the author, bought it and felt robbed.

RUBBER SOUL

Programmed, remixed, and mastered by Dexter. You can argue for this job as Dexter's best or worst. To his credit, Dexter at least had a clear concept here, which was to gather all the Beatles' records most influenced by folk-rock. "I've Just Seen a Face" becomes the opening track, not bad. But by this time, the Beatles did have intentions of their own and "Drive My Car," which opens the authentic *Rubber Soul,* conveys a completely different impression of where the band is at—there's not a comparable gutsy rocker on the entire American version. This is the first album that has an exact analogue in the Beatles' catalog in Britain (and the rest of the world, for that matter). Not a pretty sight.

"YESTERDAY" . . . AND TODAY

Not programmed, remixed, or mastered by Dexter, who'd been chased off the job on orders from London. But at this point, the American listener is really being punished by Capitol's album-creation process replacing the Beatles' own. This isn't just a hodge-podge, it's incoherent, and seems driven solely by the American company's lust to exploit the massive popularity of the ballad, "Yesterday," by Paul and the Cellos.

REVOLVER

Again, not programmed, remixed, or mastered by Dexter but he is the guiding spirit of the idiotic process. Again, the Beatles had their own vision of what the album should amount to, and this time, Capitol's re-ordering of the tracks and replacing some tracks meant for the album with others that weren't amounts to chaos. Anybody whose ear can't tell them why "And Your Bird Can Sing" provides a crucial thematic and atmospheric bridge between "Good Day Sunshine" and "For No One," need a sit-down with a 15-year-old Beatles fan—pretty much any one of us could have explained it. Yet, as with all the rest, it's still a great album.

ORIGINAL VERSIONS OF SONGS COVERED ON
THE SECOND ALBUM

Rhino Records assembled *Beatles Originals: The Original Versions of the Songs the Beatles Made Famous* in 1986. It exists only as a vinyl LP. Not to worry, however, as it contained only one song from the *Second Album*, probably for the same reasons as for the record never being released as a CD: It would cost too much in licensing and royalties. Nevertheless, the one *Second Album* song it contains is "Devil in Her Heart" by the Donays, which is not a minor matter. But if you live in a completely digital musical universe, there are other solutions.

"ROLL OVER BEETHOVEN," CHUCK BERRY

Cub Koda wrote a wonderful review of Berry's original, focusing on the music, for allmusic.com. (It's at http://www.allmusic.com/cg/amg.dll?p=amg&sql=33:hjftxcqaldje)

The song, which Koda says might have been written in response to Chuck's classically trained sister hogging the family piano, was the second charted single for Berry, reaching number 29 on the pop chart in 1956, almost a year after "Maybellene." (Two other Berry hits intervened on the R&B chart, where it climbed to number 2.) Its original LP appearance was on the soundtrack of the Alan Freed film, *Rock Rock Rock*, and it first appeared on one of the finest '50s rock'n'roll albums, *Chuck Berry Is on Top*.

"Roll Over Beethoven" was inducted into the Grammy Hall of Fame in 1989.

Allmusic.com lists 104 CDs containing versions by Berry; you could probably winnow that by almost half by omitting live versions and studio remakes he did for Mercury Records in the late 1960s. The easiest to find at time of publication is probably *20th Century Masters—The Millennium Collection: Best of Chuck Berry*, which is also budget priced. Beyond that, you can have your choice of everything from *From Andres Segovia to Jimi Hendrix: History of the Guitar from Renaissance to Rock and Roll* to *Loud Fast and Out of Control: The Wild Sounds of '50s Rock'n'Roll*, a Rhino Records box set that happens to be as good as its title.

"YOU REALLY GOT A HOLD ON ME," THE MIRACLES

The Miracles' seventh charted record, "You've Really Got a Hold on Me" was the first to crack the pop Top 10, peaking at number 8. (On the R&B chart, it made number 1.)

Its first album appearance was on *The Miracles Greatest Hits from the Beginning*, the first great Motown album (and possibly the first two-disc rock or soul LP). Allmusic.com lists 70 albums containing it, ranging from the budget (and readily available) *Forever Gold* to *Say It Loud! A Celebration of Black Music in America*, a box set. The truly ambitious can find "You Really Got a Hold On Me," along with "Please Mr. Postman" and "Money," on *The Complete Motown Singles* (Hip-O). "You've Really

Got a Hold On Me," is on disc 10, track 16, which is contained in Volume 2. (The series, whose discs are numbered consecutively, is packaged in chronological order with the discs numbered consecutively. As I write, it has reached Volume 7, disc 37, which brings it to the end of 1967.)

"DEVIL IN HIS HEART," THE DONAYS

These five albums contained the original "Devil": *American Roots of the British Invasion* (where it is the only cover song from the *Second Album* included), *British Invasion Box* (which also includes Little Richard's "Long Tall Sally"), *Kiss'n'Tell*, *Rock'n'Roll Era: Rock Classics—The Originals*, and *Rockin' On Broadway: The Time, Brent, Shad Story.*

By far the most interesting is *Rockin' On Broadway,* which basically traces the history of the independent label impresario and sometime jazz producer Bob Shad. Shad had an ear for novelty, and if you're a fan of this era's music, it's more than just useful to hear the Donays alongside such one-hit wonders as Skip and Flip's "It Was I," and the Bell Notes "I've Had It." The programming is strange though—"Bad Boy" is separated from "Devil" by Bertha Tillman's "Oh My Angel."

"MONEY (THAT'S WHAT I WANT)," BARRETT STRONG

The first Motown hit. The label was so small that when "Money" burst into the R&B top ten, peaking at number 2, the disc was switched to Anna Records, owned by

Berry Gordy's two of Gordy's sisters, Gwen and, unsurprisingly, Anna. It has forever after served as one of the company's defining songs. Set into the cover of the first volume *The Complete Motown Singles* is a 45 RPM copy of Barrett Strong's "Money."

Besides that epochal set, where it appears as track 15 on disc 1, allmusic.com lists about 50 CDs, mostly various artist compilations, that include Strong's version of "Money." Of them all, I'd recommend *20th Century Masters—The Millennium Collection: Barrett Strong*, mainly because it offers a fairly thorough survey of the music he made as a singer. A more thorough and very worthwhile disc is *The Complete Motown* Collection, a British CD. As good as he was, Strong couldn't push himself into the front ranks of the Motown roster as a vocalist. He got there as a writer, becoming Norman Whitfield's collaborator on some of the funkiest Motown hits in the late 1960s and early 1970s, including "I Heard It Through the Grapevine," "War," "Cloud Nine," and "Papa Was a Rollin' Stone."

"LONG TALL SALLY," LITTLE RICHARD

The biggest R&B hit Richard ever had, "Long Tall Sally," spent two solid months at number 1 on that chart, and reached number 6 on the pop chart. It was even certified gold for sales of 1 million or more copies, a much rarer thing in 1956 than today, when it would still be uncommon for a single song to sell that much. (It didn't hurt that the B side was "Slippin' and Slidin'," also a big hit.)

Richard made "Long Tall Sally" in New Orleans at Cosima Matassa's J&M Studio, with a great band featuring Earl Palmer on drummers, and saxophonists Lee Allen and Red Tyler. Richard recorded the song in the key of F, very high. For the Beatles version, Paul McCartney pushed himself into G, a full step higher, one of the more reckless things he's ever done with his voice. (It worked, of course.)

Allmusic.com lists more than 200 albums with Little Richard performances of "Long Tall Sally," and while he has re-recorded his hits more prolifically than most, this is also a measure of the huge popularity of the track. It's included on everything from *Max Weinberg's Let There Be Drums, Vol. 1* to *Alan Freed's Golden Picks*.

"Long Tall Sally" first appeared on an album with Richard's first LP, *Here's Little Richard*, which probably *is* the greatest rock'n'roll album of the 1950s. That album can still be found on CD, though not cheaply: It is combined with Richard's almost-equally monumental second album, *Little Richard*, on a 2006 Mobile Fidelity SACD (ultra high fidelity) disc, which even used is likely to cost more than $20.

The Georgia Peach, reissued by his original label, Specialty, in the early 1990s is not that hard to find and a used copy can be picked up cheaply. So can Specialty's *Essential Little Richard*. If you decide to pick up another Richard disc, scrutinize it carefully—you don't want the remakes he did for Vee Jay and Okeh, you want the original.

"PLEASE MR. POSTMAN," THE MARVELETTES

Also-rans in the Motown hierarchy for most of the '60s, the Marvelettes nevertheless beat every other act to number 1 on the pop charts. This massive hit also spent seven solid weeks at the top of the R&B lists.

The song was rewritten at least twice after the Marvelettes' Georgia Dobbins (who soon left the group) got it from her friend, William Garrett. Not surprisingly, the final polish was added by Brian Holland, perhaps his first Motown assignment, though he, brother Eddie Holland and Lamont Dozier would soon become the most important producers at Motown.

"Please Mr. Postman" appears on *The Complete Motown Singles Volume 1* as track 1 on disc 5. About 60 albums containing the track are listed on allmusic.com. *Motown 1's* might be the perfect way to own it, given that "Postman" is the lead track and that the *1's* concept was pioneered by the Beatles. On the other hand, you can probably find a copy of *20th Century Masters—The Millennium Collection: The Marvelettes* for about five bucks, and have their other fine hits: *"Beechwood 4-5789," "Playboy," "Too Many Fish in the Sea,"* and one of the most underrated Motown records of all, *"The Hunter Gets Captured by the Game."*

BOOKS BY DAVE MARSH

Born to Run: The Bruce Springsteen Story
The Book of Rock Lists (with Kevin Stein)
Elvis
Rocktopicon (with Sandra Choron and Debby Geller)
Before I Get Old: The Story of the Who
Fortunate Son: Criticism and Journalism by America's Best-Known Rock Writer
Trapped: Michael Jackson and the Crossover Dream
Sun City by Artists United Against Apartheid: The Making of the Record
Glory Days: Bruce Springsteen in the 1980s
The Heart of Rock & Soul: The 1001 Greatest Singles Ever Made
The New Book of Rock Lists (with James Bernard)
Louie Louie: The History and Mythology of the World's Most Famous Rock'n'Roll Song; Including the Full Details of Its Torture and Persecution at the Hands of the Kingsmen, J. Edgar Hoover's F.B.I., and a Cast of Millions; and Introducing, for the First Time Anywhere, the Actual Dirty Lyrics

Merry Christmas, Baby: Holiday Music from Bing to Sting (with Steve Propes)

The Great Rock 'n' Roll Jokebook (with Katih Kamen Goldmark)

For the Record: Sam and Dave

Two Hearts: Bruce Springsteen, The Definitive Biography 1972–2003

Forever Young: Photographs of Bob Dylan (with Douglas Gilbert)

Bruce Springsteen on Tour 1965–2005

EDITED BY DAVE MARSH

The Rolling Stone Record Guide (with John Swenson)

The New Rolling Stone Record Guide (with John Swenson)

The First Rock & Roll Confidential Report: Inside the Real World of Rock and Roll

50 Ways to Fight Censorship

Pastures of Plenty: A Self-Portrait of Woody Guthrie (with Harold Leventhal)

Heaven Is Under Our Feet (with Don Henley)

Mid-Life Confidential: The Rock Bottom Remainders Tour America with Three Chords and an Attitude

For the Record series (oral histories)

Liner Notes series